HIDDEN HISTORY
of
LAKE CHAMPLAIN

T0273890

HIDDEN HISTORY
of
LAKE CHAMPLAIN

Jason Barney and Christine Eldred

THE
History
PRESS

Published by The History Press
Charleston, SC
www.historypress.com

First published 2024

Manufactured in the United States

ISBN 9781467157254

Library of Congress Control Number: 2024931458

Dedicated to librarians—guardians of knowledge, intellectual freedom and the pleasures of reading.

Contents

ACKNOWLEDGEMENTS

W e would like to thank everyone who made this book possible: Lindsay Didio for her artistic skills and help with technology; Armand Messier for his wonderful drone images; Josh Sinz for his stylistic approach to art; newcomer Joe Smith, welcome to the team (without your creativity, these books would not be possible); and finally, thanks to Mike Kinsella for giving us the opportunity.

THE NATURAL HISTORY
OF LAKE CHAMPLAIN

On a clear, calm day, sunlight on the surface of Lake Champlain creates sparkles and flashes, glints and shadows. The color of the water shifts as it moves, in striations of blue, silver, gray and green as the surface rolls and ripples. Fed by more than a dozen rivers, the lake seldom seems still. At the water's edge, it seems to be racing to shore, arriving with a gentle splash before merging back into the flow. In fact, Lake Champlain is always flowing north, toward the Richelieu River in Quebec, ultimately joining the St. Lawrence River on its journey to the sea.

Nestled in a broad basin between New York's Adirondack Mountains and Vermont's Green Mountains, the natural history of Lake Champlain has been shaped by both geologic and human history. Both mountain ranges were created by the shifting of Earth's continental plates but through different geologic forces and in different periods. The ancestors of the Adirondack Mountains were the Grenville Mountains, an enormous chain born at least 1 billion years ago and covering a large swath of North America. Late in the life of the Grenville Mountains, a tropical sea known as the Iapetus Ocean developed, host to the world's first known coral reef and early invertebrate life forms, such as trilobites and cephalopods. About 445 million years ago, a continental shift created the Appalachian Mountain Range, including its northernmost section, the Green Mountains. The Adirondack Mountains formed later, about 165 to 85 million years ago, atop the remains of the ancient Grenville Mountains.[1]

At the end of the Last Glacial period—some fifteen thousand years ago—as the climate warmed and the glaciers shrank, melting ice flowed into the Lake Champlain Basin, creating a succession of bodies of water. The first was Lake Vermont, a freshwater glacial lake that filled the basin and its river valleys as far south as the Hudson River. About twelve thousand years ago, as the ice sheets continued to retreat north, barriers to the Atlantic Ocean melted and salt water flowed in, creating the Champlain Sea. Whales, seals, porpoises and saltwater fish inhabited the Champlain Sea, and its shoreline developed into a tundra habitat supportive of large mammals, such as mammoths, caribou and elk. Then, with the massive weight and pressure of the glaciers no longer covering the terrain, the land gradually rose in elevation, causing the Champlain Sea to become closed off from the Atlantic Ocean, making the basin once again a freshwater lake fed by precipitation and a network of rivers.[2]

The extent to which we can still see evidence of these billions of years of change is a true marvel. Amazingly, the fossil remains of invertebrates that thrived in the Iapetus Ocean Reef are visible to us in the limestone rock at D.A.R. State Park in Addison, Vermont, and on Isle La Motte, Vermont, at Goodsell Ridge Preserve and Fiske Quarry.[3] The remains of four whale species have been discovered in Quebec, the remains of a beluga whale were found in Charlotte, Vermont, and those of a hooded seal were found in Plattsburgh, New York.[4]

Humans began to inhabit the Champlain Valley some nine thousand years ago. We identify the first humans of the Champlain Valley as Paleoindians, who inhabited the area until about 7000 BCE. Paleoindians were hunters of big game animals, for in this period at the end of the glacial era, the developing tundra, grass plains and wetlands supported mammoths, mastodons, musk ox, bison, caribou, moose-elk, giant beavers, bear and deer, as well as small mammals, birds and aquatic species.[5] As the environment warmed and a boreal forest of spruce and fir replaced tundra, large animal species died out or migrated north, and it's likely humans followed them. During the next era of native history, known as the Archaic period, lasting until 900 BCE, Lake Champlain returned to a freshwater state, and the valley's woodlands transformed into a mixed deciduous forest of maple, birch, beech and oak trees.[6] Living primarily in river valleys and along the lake, Natives moved seasonally and as needed to manage their resources; they also adapted their hunting tools and techniques to catch smaller and quicker game, crafted dugout canoes for fishing and gathered nuts, berries and plants from the land.[7] The last precontact period is the Woodland period, which lasted from

Webb's Point, Shelburne Farms, Vermont. These beautiful rock formations are on display on the east side of Lake Champlain. *Library of Congress, public domain.*

900 BCE to 1600 CE. The Abenaki Natives of the Woodland era engaged in trade with other Indigenous groups, developed pottery and birchbark canoes and utilized plants, grasses and vines for nonfood resources, such as medicines, woven goods, cordage and color dyes.[8]

Evidence suggests that agriculture became part of Abenaki life in the Champlain Valley during the Woodland era, sometime between 1000 and

1450 BCE. According to Abenaki archaeologist and ethnobotanist Frederick Wiseman, archaeological digs completed near the Missisquoi River in recent years have identified the remains of corn and squash plants, sunflowers and wild rice from the Woodland period. Among the Abenaki community, it is known that beans, squash, pumpkins, Jerusalem artichokes, wild leeks, ground cherries and groundnuts (a starchy, vining tuber related to beans) were also part of their ancestral diet.[9] The Abenaki also gathered berries, tree nuts, edible ferns and wild greens and made maple syrup. Compared to agriculture in southern New England and New York, agriculture in the Champlain Valley seems to have arrived later and played a smaller role due to the area's shorter growing season.

What then was the Champlain Valley like when the first Europeans arrived? Although we might imagine the landscape prior to European settlement as a primeval forest of towering trees, uniformly large, ancient trees were not typical of the Champlain Valley. Our notion of an old-growth forest tends to be shaped by the mythic qualities of the western U.S. landscape, where species such as redwoods, Douglas fir and Ponderosa pine can live for thousands of years, growing into giants. But trees native to the forests of

Split Rock Mountain. These unique rocks are located on the New York side of Lake Champlain. *Library of Congress, public domain.*

the Northeast are comparatively smaller and have shorter lifespans, in the range of fifty to four hundred years. Studies of bogs, marshes and soil layers, in combination with details from historic records, show that the trees of the seventeenth-century northern forest were a varied mix of ages, sizes and species, reflecting regular cycles of disruption and regrowth. Environmental forces, including fires, storms, high winds, climatic shifts and competition between species periodically damaged or altered forest ecosystems, initiating processes of succession, in which newly exposed areas were populated by scrubby and fast-growing vegetation and then succeeded in time by slower-growing trees, layered forest floors and shade canopies.[10]

Samuel de Champlain, a Frenchman who helped establish the colony of New France in eastern Canada, was the first European to map and describe Lake Champlain. Escorted by sixty Montagnais Native allies, Champlain first ventured on to Lake Champlain in July 1609. Reaching the northern entrance to the lake, Samuel de Champlain described, in vivid language, the bounty of the land.

> We departed on the following day, pursuing our way up the river as far as the entrance to the lake. In it are many beautiful low islands covered with very fine woods and meadows with much wild fowl and animals to hunt, such as stags, fallow deer, fawns, roebucks, bears, and other kinds of animals which come from the mainland to these islands. We caught there a great many of them. There are also many beavers, both in that river and in several small streams which fall into it. This region although pleasant is not inhabited by Indians, on account of their wars; for they withdraw from the rivers as far as they can into the interior, in order not to be easily surprised.
>
> On the following day we entered the lake which is some 80 or 100 leagues in length; In which I saw four beautiful islands about ten, twelve, and fifteen leagues in length, which, like the Iroquois river were formerly inhabited by Indians: but they have been abandoned, since they have been at war with one another. There are also several rivers flowing into the lake, on whose banks are many fine trees of the same varieties we have in France, with many of the finest vines I had seen anywhere. There are many chestnut trees which I had only seen on the shore of this lake in which there is also a great abundance of many species of fish.…
>
> Continuing our way along this lake in a westerly direction and viewing the country, I saw towards the East very high mountains on the tops of which there was snow. I enquired [sic] of the natives whether these parts

The flora and fauna of Lake Champlain are some of the most beautiful in the country. *Library of Congress, public domain.*

were inhabited. They said they were, and by the Iroquois, and that in those parts there were beautiful valleys and fields rich in corn such as I have eaten in that country, along with other products in abundance. And they said that the lake went close to the mountains, which as I judged might be some 25 leagues away from us. [11]

While European settlement drastically changed the Champlain Valley in innumerable ways, Natives also shaped the land to suit their needs, particularly as agricultural methods developed. The ecosystem of the Champlain Valley is markedly different than it was in 1609. Species such as chestnut trees, American elms, mountain lions (often called catamounts in this region), wolves, caribou, elk and passenger pigeons were once abundant but have gone extinct or disappeared due to hunting, disease, deforestation and habitat loss. Many other animal species that had been extirpated from the region by the mid-nineteenth century have been reintroduced in the last one hundred years; these species include beavers, deer, moose, black bears, bald eagles, ospreys, peregrine falcons, wild turkeys, grouse, otters, fishers, martens, Canada geese, loons and lynx. [12] Industrial and agricultural chemicals and waste runoff have harmed the health and quality of the entire Lake Champlain Watershed. Invasive plant and insect species have altered the ecosystem of the lake, as well as those of wetlands, forests and fields. Surprisingly, some of the species that are now most familiar to us are not native to North America, including earth worms, honeybees, dandelions, burdock, apple trees, garden snails, house finches, house sparrows, pigeons and starlings.

2

THE FRENCH ERA

For the colony of New France, Lake Champlain was a wilderness frontier far from its early settlements along the Atlantic coast and St. Lawrence River Delta. Nevertheless, for 150 years, the Champlain Valley was vital to French strategic and economic interests. Although the French attempted to lay claim to the lake and its fertile valley, they were able to establish only a few small and isolated villages there, the largest ones springing up around military fortifications at the southern end of Lake Champlain.

Lake Champlain was an important corridor of trade and transportation and, flanked by mountain ranges on both sides, acted as a natural boundary for several nations, both Indigenous and European.[13] The area's Native communities, including the Mohawks, Mahicans and Abenaki, had lived and moved through the Champlain Valley for thousands of years, sometimes warring with each other, but all gradually found their homelands and peoples at the crossroads of economic and political conflict with European powers. England, France and, to a lesser degree, the Netherlands (which controled the Manhattan and the Hudson Valley until 1664) all desired to access and control the lake and its resources for their own needs. The lucrative European market for beaver pelts and other furs created intense economic competition among all parties, disrupting Indigenous economies and environments and creating new territorial and political conflicts. As the French pushed west in their search for furs, Lake Champlain was a critical byway that connected New France to the trading posts and markets of New England and the

Hudson River Valley. In addition, the lake supported abundant river habitats for beavers and other fur-bearing animals and provided easier access into the Adirondack and Green Mountains.[14]

Early on, the French learned that the Champlain Valley was also a back door into their fledgling colony, allowing warring parties easy access to the interior of their territory. In Champlain's only visit to the lake, his Algonquin allies asked him to join them in a battle against the Mohawk—a nation that was part of the Iroquois confederacy—in the area of present-day Ticonderoga, New York. Although he had no personal stake in the conflict, Champlain was eager to demonstrate his support for the Algonquins and used a firearm to devastating effect, killing two Iroquois chiefs.[15] Just as there was a history of conflict and competition between England and France, the Iroquois confederacy and the Algonquin nations had also been at war. Over time, military alliances formed between the Dutch and Mahicans, the English and the Iroquois, and the French and Algonquins and Abenaki. As cycles of violence and retaliation occurred, New France found itself frequently vulnerable to attack by British and Indigenous enemies approaching from Lake Champlain and the Richelieu River.

Throughout the existence of New France, its population was quite small and homogeneous when compared to that of the English and Dutch colonies, which grew rapidly with the influx of religious exiles, like the Puritans, Quakers, Mennonites, Jews and Huguenots, as well as those seeking opportunities to acquire land and wealth. New France's first administrators were fur traders who were granted a monopoly by the king, and their focus was on extracting resources from the colony. France specifically prohibited non-Catholics from migrating to New France, preferring to offer economic opportunity to Catholics.[16] Catholic clergy, particularly Jesuit missionaries who sought to convert Natives, had a strong and early presence in New France but did not marry and have families who would add to the colony's numbers. Making a life in the harsh wilderness of North America held little appeal to the French, and persistent attacks by the Iroquois effectively kept further settlement in check. New France's first census in 1666 showed that its population was around only 3,200, while New England had a population ten times the size and New Netherland had grown to have some 9,000 colonists.[17]

After the Dutch ceded their colony to the British in 1667, confrontation between England and France over land became inevitable, and the Lake Champlain region was a key battleground. Each side watched the other warily. The English extended their land patents north from Manhattan, creating large tracts for settlement on the southwestern side of Lake

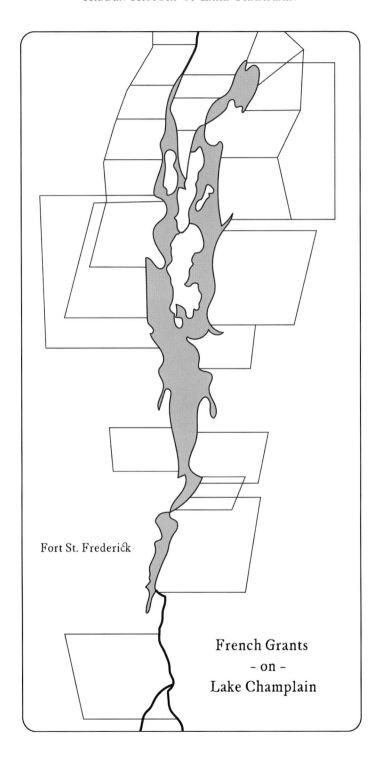

Fort St. Frederick

French Grants
- on -
Lake Champlain

Champlain near present-day Lake George and Ticonderoga and along the Hudson River from Albany to Saratoga. This region contained several fortifications, including Fort Anne, Fort Edward and the important Dutch fur trading post of Fort Orange, known today as Albany.[18]

At the same time, after decades of royal neglect, King Louis XIV turned his attention to New France. To expand the fur trade and hold territory, the French needed to grow their population and successfully defend it from enemies. First, the king ended the colony's governance by merchant monopolies and transformed it into a royal colony administered by appointees. Over ten years, from 1663 to 1673, the king sent about eight hundred young women, known as the King's Daughters—often poor women and orphans—to New France to help create families that would grow the colony. The first large military force, a contingent of one thousand experienced French soldiers, was provided to build and operate a series of fortifications at strategic points throughout New France. Just like England, France sought to stake a claim and exert control in the Champlain Valley. After creating fortifications along the Richelieu River above Lake Champlain, New France's governor then sought a location on the lake itself that would allow for greater control of access to New France from the Champlain Valley. The first site chosen was located on present-day Isle La Motte, where Fort Sainte-Anne was established in 1666.

Opposite: A map depicting the original French land grants along Lake Champlain. *Artwork by Lindsay Didio.*

Above: An early depiction of what an early French homestead would have looked like. *Cornelius Krieghoff, public domain.*

A lull in active conflict followed, leaving Fort Sainte-Anne abandoned by 1671, but the site remained a frequent stopping point for French forces and other travelers on Lake Champlain.[19]

By 1673, the population of New France had doubled to more than 6,700, but most residents remained clustered in existing towns and villages.[20] During the 1730s and 1740s, under Louis XV, the French Crown issued a series of twenty large land grants around Lake Champlain, hoping to encourage greater settlement and agricultural growth.[21] Lands were granted under the French seigneurial system, in which a designated landholder known as a *seigneur* was granted a large tract of land and was responsible for subdividing it and finding people to clear, cultivate and settle it. In exchange for the land, the seigneur gave the king his loyalty, paid taxes, provided military service and committed to organizing workers for several days to work on projects like road building.[22]

The French style of land cultivation was known as ribbon farming. Compared to the English style of agriculture, the French farmed in long, narrow strips often fronted by a river, lake or stream. Such an arrangement gave each farmer access to a variety of land types, from fertile valley soils to the resources of the forest, giving rise to farms of diversified crops and products. Ribbon farming also meant that homesteads along the shore would be closer together, providing greater protection and visibility.[23]

The Champlain Valley's seigneuries were awarded to the military leaders, shipbuilders, merchants and administrators of New France—men whose work the king wished to reward and whom he believed had the ambition and leadership skills to realize his vision for growth. However, it proved extremely difficult to entice French immigrants to settle in remote areas far from the existing centers of trade and community, and most seigneuries remained untouched. Some fledgling settlements, such as Grand Isle and Malletts Bay in present-day Colchester, Vermont were reportedly abandoned after being burned by the English and Iroquois forces in 1744, during King George's War.[24] It appears there were three seigneuries along Lake Champlain with notable settlement during the final twenty years of the existence of New France: Swanton, Vermont; Alburgh, Vermont; and Chimney Point in Addison, Vermont.[25]

Swanton, along the falls of the Missisquoi River, was known to be an Abenaki village, although, due to wars and epidemics, the Abenaki periodically withdrew north to live in St. Francis. By 1742, a few hundred Abenaki were living there again, and the Jesuits had built a small chapel to serve the Missisquoi Mission. Swanton was part of the St. Armand seigneurie, granted in 1748 to René-Nicolas Levasseur, a shipbuilder and logger for King Louis XV. The following year, Levasseur built a sawmill at the foot of the Missisquoi River falls. On a hill near the mill, a stockade was constructed for protection. A village of some fifty homes and a stone church eventually formed a small community of both French and Abenaki. The villagers cultivated fields and planted orchards, worked at the sawmill and in the forests and worshipped at the mission chapel. Although the British burned the sawmill in the fall of 1757 and New France was defeated in 1759, the Swanton settlement, including the Jesuit mission, endured and grew under British rule.[26]

Alburgh was part of the Seigneury of Foucault, granted to François Foucault, a Quebec merchant and financier. The primary location that was developed was a prominent point on the lake named Pointe du Détour, known today as Windmill Point, a name that likely reflects the traces of French settlement that were visible there for some decades. Historian Guy Coolidge described the community in his book *The French Occupation of the Champlain Valley from 1609 to 1759*:

> *In 1740, there were eight settlers to form the nucleus of the little village planned by M. de Foucault; the following year, a stone mill costing 4,000 livres was built near the lake shore, three new settlers joining the settlement; a church 20 by 40 feet was begun by M. de Foucault to be completed in the spring ready for the arrival of the missionary. In addition, the proprietor had made free grant to the Bishop of Quebec of a plot two "arpents" front by forty arpents depth, comprising the site of the church and the priest's house with sufficient land for farming and for setting off a cemetery.*[27]

Like Mallett's Bay and Grand Isle, the French village at Alburgh appears to have been destroyed a few years after it was established. Swedish botanist Peter Kalm, while visiting the lake in July 1749, several months after the conclusion of King George's War, recorded "a windmill, built of stone, stands on the east side of the lake on a projecting piece of ground. Some Frenchmen have lived near it; they left it when the war broke out (1744), and are not yet to come back to it. The English, with their Indians, have burned the houses here several times, but the mill remained unhurt."[28]

The most significant colonial French presence in the Champlain Valley came with the construction and staffing of military installations on strategic points at the southern end of the lake. At a location called Pointe à la Chevelure, prominent points of land on both the eastern and western sides narrow the lake considerably, forming an excellent location for military defense. Because of its advantageous position, the spot had long been used as a rough trading post and scouting location.[29] In 1731, the French built a stockade on the eastern side at the location known today as Chimney Point. On the western shore, the construction of a large stone fort began in 1734 and was completed in 1737. The French named it Fort St. Frédéric, but it is known today by the name the British used, Crown Point. Ten years later and ten miles to the south, the French built the even larger Fort Carillon between 1755 and 1758. Familiar to us as Fort Ticonderoga, Fort Carillon was barely completed when the French lost their hold on New France, and it fell into the hands of the British. Therefore, Fort St. Frédéric and Chimney Point, which faced each other across the lake, formed the most extensive French settlement in the southern Champlain Valley.

Coolidge's research showed, "The garrison was generally composed of 120 men; on both sides of the lake land grants grew in number; the two villages opposite the Pointe à la Chevelure opposite the fort spread north and south; the vicinity of the fort became dotted with cultivated plots of land, kitchen-gardens and small homes; there was a priest in residence to minister to the needs of the growing settlements."[30] He wrote that at least two cemeteries had been established during the twenty-eight-year lifespan

Hidden by the passage of the centuries, we may never know the true extent of the early French settlement along Lake Champlain. *Cornelius_Krieghoff, public domain.*

of the villages and detailed parish records that were preserved by the fort's priests, which show 243 baptisms, 31 marriages and 198 deaths occurred.[31]

The success of the settlement around Fort St. Frédéric was no doubt due to the protection and the population associated with the fort itself. Soldiers were encouraged to stay and settle as farmers after their service was complete and were given much assistance and financial incentive to do so. Peter Kalm stayed at Fort St. Frédéric during his travels on Lake Champlain in 1750 and described the life of the typical French soldier stationed there as well as those veterans who stayed on to settle the land:

> *July the 6th. Veterans cottages. The soldiers who had been paid off after the war* [King George's War, 1744–48] *had built houses around the fort on the grounds allotted to them; but most of these habitations were no more than wretched cottages, no better than those in the most wretched places of Sweden. There was that difference, however, that the inhabitants here were rarely oppressed by hunger, and could eat good bread and pure wheat bread. The huts which they had erected consisted of boards, standing perpendicularly close to each other. The roofs were of wood too. The crevices were stopped up with clay to keep the room warm. The floor was usually clay, or a black limestone, which is common here....*
>
> *July the 10th...A Soldiers Rations. The soldiery enjoys such advantages here as they are not allowed in any part of the world. Those who formed the garrison of this place had a very plentiful allowance from their government. They get every day a pound and a half of wheat bread, which is almost more than they can eat. They likewise get plenty of peas, bacon, and salt or dried meat. Sometimes they kill oxen and other cattle, the flesh of which is distributed among the soldiers. All the officers kept cows, at the expense of the king, and the milk they gave was more than sufficient to supply them. The soldiers had each a small garden outside the fort, which they were allowed to attend and to plant in it whatever they liked. Some of them had built summer houses in them and planted all kinds of vegetables. The governor told me that it was a general custom to allow the soldiers a plot of ground for kitchen gardens at...the French forts hereabouts as were not situated near great towns, from whence they could be supplied. In time of peace, the soldiers have very little guard duty when at the fort; and as the lake close by was full of fish, and the woods abounded with birds and animals, those amongst them who chose to be diligent could leave live extremely well and like a lord in regard to food. Each soldier got a new coat every two years; but annually, a waistcoat, cap, hat, breeches, cravat,*

two pair of stockings, two pair of shoes, and as much wood as he had occasion for in winter. They likewise got five sols apiece every day, which is augmented to thirty sols when they have any particular labor for the king. When this is considered it is not surprising to find the men are very healthy, well fed, strong and lively here. When a soldier falls sick he is brought to the hospital, where the king provides him with a bed, food, medicine, and people to take care of and serve him....

The soldiers who are sent hither from France commonly served till they are forty or fifty years old, after which they are honorably discharged and allowed to settle upon and cultivate a piece of ground....Those who are born here commonly agreed to serve the crown during six, eight, or ten years after which they are discharged and settled down as farmers in this country. The king presents each discharged soldier with a piece of land, being commonly 40 arpents long and but three broad, if the soil be of equal goodness throughout; but they get somewhat more if it be poorer. As soon as a soldier settles to cultivate such a piece of land, he is at first assisted by the king, who supplies him, his wife and children with provisions during the first three or four years. The king likewise gives him a cow and the most necessary instruments for agriculture. Some soldiers are sent to assist him in building a house, for which the king pays them. These are of great help to a poor man who begins to keep house, and it seems that in a country where the troops are so highly, distinguished by royal favor, the king cannot be at a loss for soldiers. For the better cultivation and population of Canada, a plan was proposed some years ago for sending three hundred men over from France every year, by which means the old soldiers might always be retired, marry and settle in the country. The land which was allotted to the soldiers about this place, was very good, consisting throughout of a deep mold, mixed with clay.

The soil about Fort St. Frederic is said to be very fertile, on both sides of the river, and before the last war a great many French families, especially old soldiers, settled there, but the king obliged them to go into Canada, or to settle close to the Fort, and sleep in it at night. A great number of them returned at this time, and it was thought that about 40 or 50 families would go to settle here this autumn.

By the 1750s, the British colonies had more than 1.5 million residents, while New France had less than 30,000.[32] In 1759, New France was ultimately worn down by the British military, with its greater numbers of soldiers and its superior navy, which restricted the movement of food, supplies and soldiers into and out of Quebec. Although the French had only a tenuous foothold in the area of Lake Champlain during the colonial era, thousands of their descendants chose to emigrate there in the nineteenth and twentieth centuries, becoming an integral part of the culture and community of the Champlain Valley.

3

THE REVOLUTIONARY WAR ERA

I t is difficult to visualize history that unfolded 250 years ago. The Champlain Valley was a hotbed of activity during the Revolutionary War. History textbooks focus on the writings and actions of the founding fathers and the major battles, like Lexington and Concord, Bunker Hill and Saratoga. However, much of the War for Independence unfolded on Lake Champlain. Much of that patriotic history is hidden.

One of the more interesting gems from that era was a structure that, for the most part, no longer exits. It was the first bridge that connected Vermont and New York. It was an impressive engineering accomplishment, and its location is a protected historic site.

In the summer of 1776, the Revolution was not going well for the colonials. More than a year had passed since the early successes of the Battles of Lexington and Concord and the seizing of Fort Ticonderoga. Further achievements followed, as the colonials invaded and occupied Quebec. The British retreated to Quebec City.

What followed was a disaster. British reinforcements arrived, and the American army stumbled, retreated and collapsed. By July 1776, the rebels had fallen back to the southern portions of the lake, licking their wounds. Exhausted, smallpox-infested soldiers looked north and knew only the lake separated them from the British. To stave off the enemy, the gears of war turned, and ingenuity helped the American cause.

Benedict Arnold began constructing a fleet to hold off the most powerful navy in the world. The area's existing fortifications were evaluated. Crown

Point, located in the south-central part of the lake, was out of date. If the British came over water, they could be observed from that location. A lot of energy was put into repairing Fort Ticonderoga. It had been constructed in the 1750s and was now twenty years old. It was in bad shape.

The Vermont side of the lake also received attention. In July, construction began on another fort, dubbed "Mount Independence." When it was completed, the colonials could defend both shores. The engineering work was designed by Jedathun Baldwin. Colonial generals tasked him with building the defensive structures to hold off the British. Baldwin believed that together, both locations might be enough to repel the enemy. He feared they could not function independently. Either side might be isolated or destroyed by a determined British force. Communication across the lake presented dangerous delays.

Baldwin knew this was an impossible situation. Colonial soldiers needed to be able to reinforce either side quickly. He decided there needed to be a bridge. The engineers didn't have massive trucks to bring construction materials. They didn't have concrete. They just had the tools of the era. They used oxen, horses and boats to move equipment. It was a massive project.

A lot of lumber was needed. Crews were sent into the woods and ordered to bring down large trees that would become support beams. Men sawed and felled the trees, and oxen dragged them to the lake shore. Getting them in place was not easy. Baldwin analyzed how the logs could be lowered into the water without floating away. They had to be submerged and held in place in water that was approximately twenty feet deep.

From the ice in late spring and ships when the ice went out, Baldwin ordered his men to drop large rocks and boulders to the lake bottom. They landed in prearranged spots, an impossibly precise task. Once the beams were in place, engineers made sure they extended high enough above the water.[33] The planking for the bridge was added last. When it was completed, the bridge was an engineering accomplishment.

The British made their move in the fall of 1776. Colonial leadership sent large numbers of reinforcements to Ticonderoga and Mount Independence. It was the largest American army in the colonies at that time.

It was needed.

In October, the British navy defeated Benedict Arnold's fleet at the Battle of Valcour, and they probed into the southern areas of the Champlain Valley. Thousands of British, Hessian and Native allies approached Ticonderoga, Mount Independence and the indispensable footbridge that connected them. They were itching for a fight, but the cold season had set in. The

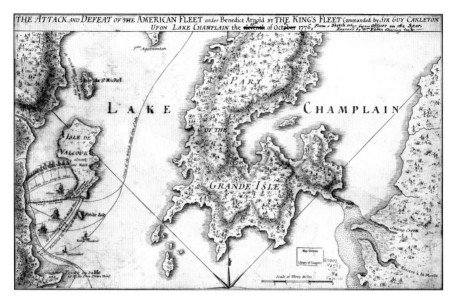

Valcour Island was the location of one of the most significant battles in American history. *Library of Congress, public domain.*

redcoats assessed the large force in front of them, weighed the risks of an assault and pulled back to Quebec. Preparations for an even larger attack were made for the next year.

The ambitious General Johnny Burgoyne commanded a larger British force of nearly ten thousand in 1777. Aware that the Americans had redeployed units from Ticonderoga and Mount Independence to help Washington's army move south, the British were confident they could retake the Champlain Valley, now defended by only a few thousand rebel soldiers. In late June, the British army and navy were once again on the lake. In early July, they fanned out on the east and western shores of Lake Champlain, wanting to encircle the smaller American force.

General Arthur St. Clair, the American commander, considered a retreat. It was better to save his army than risk a siege. The British placed cannons on the high ground to the west of Fort Ticonderoga, and Hessian soldiers were on land, moving south and east toward Mount Independence. St. Clair's colonial army would be lost if he waited too long.

The footbridge that Jedathun Baldwin's engineers constructed became the indispensable escape route for the American army. On July 5, the colonials defending Ticonderoga abandoned the fort and fled across the bridge. Their retreat occurred under the veil of darkness and was not well organized, but the Americans had their escape route. They walked softly and avoided using lights to evade detection. Mount Independence was also abandoned, and the British were just hours behind. The Americans lived to fight another day.

That day came sooner than they hoped.

They moved southeast for a full day and night; the British pursued. The main colonial force made it through the Vermont towns of Brandon and Pittsford and then moved toward Castleton and Rutland. The rear guard stopped to rest in Hubbardton. On the morning of July 7, the British arrived, and the only major Revolutionary War engagement to occur on Vermont soil ensued. During the following critical weeks, British battalions were defeated at the Battle of Bennington, and the entire British force was eventually defeated at the Battle of Saratoga.

The situation in the Champlain Valley became much calmer. The war was still raging, with constant raids and strikes carried out by both sides. However, Ticonderoga, Mount Independence and the connecting footbridge were used much less than they had been earlier in the war.

The Revolutionary War ended. Time passed. Years went by.

Today, historians, archaeologists and public officials work to preserve the historical importance of these many locations. Fort Ticonderoga, by far, receives the most attention. The old, damaged fort has been rebuilt and

The English presence on Lake Champlain was significant during the Revolutionary War. *Library of Congress, public domain.*

Fort Ticonderoga was a critically important location during the Revolutionary War. *Photograph by Jason Barney.*

serves as a very popular tourist attraction. On the Vermont side, officials proudly link and preserve what remains of Mount Independence, which was critically important to the defense of the Champlain Valley.

And between them, remnants of the old bridge remain—hidden.

All that rested above water, the walkway between the two strategically important locations, is now gone. What remains is obscured by the depths of Lake Champlain. Boaters pass over it daily. Tourists read about it and wonder. The structural supports and posts remain, and occasionally, sections come loose and wash up on shore. The bridge remains hidden in the past, shrouded by the depths of the beloved lake.

4

ST. ANNE'S SHRINE

S t. Anne's Shrine is a Roman Catholic religious retreat on the northwest shore of Isle La Motte in the Champlain Islands. A peaceful and verdant spot with a view of New York's Adirondack Mountains, the shrine is active in the summer and attracts thousands of visitors. First erected in 1892, the shrine's location has a 450-year-old history as the site of Fort Sainte-Anne, built in 1666 by the government of New France to protect its colony from British and Iroquois attacks by way of Lake Champlain. Before that, it was known to the French Jesuit missionaries as place where the Abenaki and Iroquois camped.[34] Its role today as a site of Catholic pilgrimage and a shrine to Saint Anne is intimately linked to the enduring presence of the French in the Champlain Valley.

It is said that Fort St. Anne was the site of the first Catholic mass in the Champlain Valley—and perhaps in all the northeastern United States. The fort was built in the summer of 1666 by about three hundred men, mostly soldiers of the Carignan-Salières Regiment, under the guidance of Captain Pierre de la Motte. Based on similar forts of the time, it is believed that Fort St. Anne was fairly small—about 144 feet long by 96 feet wide—and designed with a double palisade and four bastions. Inside the fort's enclosure were a forge, well, brick oven and chapel. Reachable only by water, Fort St. Anne was an isolated place, desolate in winter and situated close to Iroquois territory, far from Quebec's settlements.[35]

In July 1666, the fort was completed and dedicated to Saint Anne, an important saint to the French, particularly in the region of Brittany. Saint

A winter view of St. Anne's Shrine on the west coast of Isle La Motte. Frozen Lake Champlain and New York are visible in the distance. *Photograph by Armand Messier, Northern Vermont Aerial Photography.*

Anne is the mother of the Virgin Mary and the patron saint of Quebec Province, as well as patroness of women, educators, carpenters and miners. She is venerated by the French and a source of inspiration particularly for the Edmundite order.[36]

The first winter at Fort St. Anne proved to be a brutal one. Food was insufficient and what was available was of poor quality. The soldiers' diet primarily consisted of salted meat and bread made from flour that had spoiled. Scurvy was prevalent, causing great suffering and leaving the soldiers at the colony's most remote outpost in a weakened and vulnerable state. Once the fort's difficulties became known, a Sulpician monk from Marieville (Montreal) was sent to minister to the soldiers. The monk, Francois Dollier de Casson, later wrote about the experience.

Dollier arrived on snowshoes, carrying a heavy pack with an injured knee. He was escorted by a few soldiers from another French fort he had sheltered at along the way. En route, one of the soldiers fell through the ice on Lake Champlain and was rescued from drowning by Dollier and the commanding officer. On their arrival at Fort St. Anne, they were greeted with joy and relief by Captain La Motte and his officers, but Dollier immediately found that the conditions there were dire. Forty soldiers were ill with scurvy. Some had died just that day, while others were close to death and desperately hoping he would arrive in time to give them the sacrament of last rites. Dollier arranged for his escorts to take one ill man to the hospital at Marieville. The Sulpicians in Montreal then sent food to the fort, urgently delivered by sledge over ice and snow, undoubtedly saving the lives of the men. Included among the food were dried fruits and fresh vegetables, such as prunes and French purslane, a highly nutritious cultivated green. At the time, it was not known that a lack of vitamin C in the diet was the cause of scurvy.

For three months, Dollier nursed the sick and cared for the dying at Fort St. Anne before he returned to Marieville when the illness abated in the spring. After learning of the soldiers' sufferings, the Bishop of Quebec visited Fort St. Anne the following summer. Traveling by birch bark canoe, Bishop Francois de Laval performed mass at the fort and gave confirmation to a group of Natives who had converted to Christianity.[37]

The French had abandoned Fort St. Anne by 1671, during a period of relative peace in the Champlain Valley. But it remained an important stopping point for parties traveling up and down the lake; it was also a staging ground for troop movements on Lake Champlain throughout the later wars and conflicts of the seventeenth and eighteenth centuries.

St. Anne's Shrine has been a special place for Catholics since its first services in 1666.
Photograph by Armand Messier, Northern Vermont Aerial Photography.

After the fall of New France in 1759, the British marked the boundary between Quebec and New England at the forty-fifth parallel. Isle La Motte fell below the borderline but was not yet part of Vermont. Vermont did not exist, for its land was in dispute—the territory claimed by both New Hampshire and New York. The dispute was not settled until after the American Revolution. In 1790, Vermont, which included the Champlain Islands, achieved statehood.

In 1853, as French Canadian and Irish immigration to the region steadily increased, Louis de Goesbriand was named the Catholic Church's first bishop of Vermont. Bishop De Goesbriand was a Breton and sought to revive interest in Saint Anne among his parishioners. In 1886, a Catholic parish was established that included Alburg, Isle La Motte and North Hero. An early parish priest, Reverend Joseph Kerlidou, performed extensive historical and on-site research into the location of the old fort. The Vermont Diocese wished to reclaim the land that had been consecrated two hundred years earlier, honoring the spiritual work undertaken by their brethren in the wilderness of the Champlain Valley.

In 1892, the diocese purchased a parcel of land that was once part of the old Fort St. Anne and erected a small chapel. A statue of St. Anne created

Catholic services are held at St. Anne's Shrine during the summer. *Photograph by Armand Messier, Northern Vermont Aerial Photography.*

in Montreal was installed and still graces the chapel today. The following summer, some two thousand people came, many traveling by steamboat, to attend the blessing of the new chapel. Soon after, pilgrimages to the shrine by steamboat on Lake Champlain became a popular summer excursion.

St. Anne's Shrine was purchased by the Society of St. Edmund Fathers in 1921 and has been managed by them ever since. The Edmundite Fathers built the open-air chapel and pavilion that the shrine is well known for today and have continued to add facilities and services that allow for meetings, retreats and religious services for sizable groups. Also founders of St. Michael's College in Winooski, Vermont, the Edmundites maintain a strong connection between the college and the shrine.[38]

Today, Saint Anne's Shrine remains popular with both tourists and pilgrims. In the summer months, mass is held in the open-air pavilion, and the feast of St. Anne is celebrated each July. The shrine has a cafeteria, gift shop and gathering hall. Camping is available, along with cabins for those staying on retreat. Gardens and statues offer contemplative spaces, and a pleasant park near the water's edge is accessible to the public for picnics and swimming. Near the shore is a large statue of Samuel de Champlain and an Algonquin ally, created during Expo 67 (a world's fair held in Montreal in 1967) and given to the town of Isle La Motte in 1968. The location of the old Fort St. Anne is marked on the shrine's Way of Calvary.

5
FORTS

Ticonderoga, Crown Point, Montgomery and Isle Aux Noix

L ake Champlain's military history is unique and unmatched in North America. Over the centuries, it has hosted armies, navies, invasions and raids. It is difficult for people living in the early twenty-first century to imagine how important it was.

As a result of this lore, people can experience the most impressive fortification in North America, Fort Ticonderoga. Its massive, star-shaped stone walls are unforgettable. However, it didn't look like it does now two centuries ago, when its military use was over.

In the middle of the lake, travelers drive the Crown Point Bridge, which connects Vermont and New York. The Chimney Point Historic Site rests on the Vermont side, which provides a plethora of information about groups who inhabited the region through time. From different Indigenous peoples to the first French settlers and the English and Americans, the site is steeped with history. Just to the west, across the open water, are the Crown Point ruins. Much of the old structure no longer exists, but the classic defensive fortifications remain. The French called the location Fort St. Frederic.

Along the Canadian border rest the very visible but now-crumbling remains of Fort Montgomery. Locals inappropriately identify it as "Fort Blunder" because its construction started on the Canadian side of the border. That was corrected, and stones were properly placed on the American side. It was never used during a time of war. Within Quebec and in the confines of the Richelieu River lay the impressive but isolated

The Fort Ticonderoga that people visit today is much different than the original, as it has gone through years of neglect. *Library of Congress, public domain.*

Isle Aux Noix. Many Americans are not even aware of its existence. Today, it is known as Fort Lennox.

Each of these locations has a unique story obscured by the fog of time.

Most French colonists settled along the St. Lawrence River in Montreal and Quebec City. As the colony expanded, they traveled south to the Richelieu River and then into Lake Champlain. The English settled much farther south, along New England's Atlantic coast. Time passed, and the British colonies became larger. They expanded northward. War had ravaged Europe for centuries, and that conflict spilled over into North America.

To keep the New England colonies at arm's length, the French embraced having a permanent military presence on Lake Champlain. The location of their first fortifications were what we know as Chimney Point and Crown Point. Chimney Point was small and temporary. Fort St. Frederic was larger and much more substantial and was completed in the 1730s. Numerous wars occurred, and by the 1750s, the French realized they needed a larger presence on the lake. Once Fort Carillon was completed, the English were determined to eliminate the threat to the north. The British colonial

Before the fort was repaired and restored, some parts lay in ruins. *Library of Congress, public domain.*

The walls of Fort Ticonderoga were impressive during each decade. *Library of Congress, public domain.*

populations outnumbered the French significantly. If the British could push into Champlain Valley and challenge the French on Lake Champlain, the French possessions in North America might fall.

The French realized this. They maintained their presence at Fort Saint Frederic and bolstered their forces at Carillon. At its peak, it was the most important fortress in North America. The French used it as a base and attacked British held territory near Lake George in 1757.

The first time the English moved against Carillon in 1758, it was a disaster. The second assault occurred in 1759, and the result was much different.

Approximately 12,000 British soldiers and colonial militia approached Carillon's 3,500 French defenders. The French realized their precarious situation and decided to destroy everything they had built. In late July 1759, before falling back to the north, toward Fort St. Frederic, they set explosives and obliterated much of the fort. They did not want the British to gain control of such a valuable location. The French destroyed Fort St. Fredric about a week after Fort Carillon fell to the enemy. Their last-ditch effort to hold off the British came when they fortified Isle Aux Noix, just north of Alburgh and Missisquoi Bay. Isle Aux Noix was described by some Frenchmen as the most important location in New France. Their situation was desperate—it was akin to trying to build trenches to hold off an oncoming tidal wave. It was during these final stages of the war that ruins of Fort Carillon were rebuilt by the British. It was renamed Fort Ticonderoga.

The final assault came in August 1760. The British landed forces on the east side of the Richelieu River and set up their own cannons. Their guns were able to bombard any retreat north. The French pulled back under the cover of darkness, and the British wave pushed north, conquering Montreal and capturing all of France's holdings in North America. The British initiated substantial repairs on the Lake Champlain forts.

They considered the possibility that the area might again become the focal point in future wars. Repairs, upgrades and alterations were made at Fort Ticonderoga. Rather than rebuild Fort St. Frederic, they constructed something bigger but less complex, a mere base of operations, Crown Point.

Isle Aux Noix was virtually abandoned.

Peace settled across the land, but New England colonial ambitions boiled over in the 1770s. By 1773, when a chimney fire destroyed much of the barracks at Crown Point, there was only a small number of British soldiers garrisoned there. The next year, engineers and planners questioned the necessity of keeping any forces at Crown Point.

The ruins at Crown Point. *Library of Congress, public domain.*

Even Ticonderoga was hardly maintained. By the outbreak of the American Revolution, much of it was unusable. Its walls were failing and in desperate need of repair.

All three locations received attention during the American Revolution, but the fighting in the northeast spanned only three years, from 1776 to 1779. Ticonderoga was strategically important for the colonial invasion of Quebec, but the fort's cannons were much more valuable. Crown Point was used by the Americans but became a small hub in the resupply chain. Isle Aux Noix received upgrades by the British but was taken and then abandoned by the Americans when their invasion failed. In 1777, when the British swept through the Champlain Valley, they had little interest in putting massive resources into repairs. After the Saratoga campaign, only limited numbers of fighting men were in the area anyway.

By the War of 1812, most of the old forts were useless. As that conflict began, Burlington and Plattsburgh were better bases. The British upgraded and defended Isle Aux Noix, but the Americans discarded Ticonderoga and Crown Point as relics. After that war, the British maintained a presence at Isle Aux Noix, but the growing network of roads made it obsolete.

As a military installation and then as a historic site, Fort Ticonderoga received major repairs. Crown Point did not. *Library of Congress, public domain.*

As a strategic location, Crown Point was the perfect place to keep watch over Lake Champlain. *Library of Congress, public domain.*

Fort Ticonderoga today, a monument to Lake Champlain's unique history. *Public domain.*

The strategic mindset that the old forts represented was not lost on the American government. If the British maintained a force at Isle Aux Noix, it could always be used against America.

So, the American military decided to show the flag close to Canada. Even though the two countries became friendlier and culturally closer, the Americans began the construction of Fort Montgomery in 1816 at the extreme northwestern point of Lake Champlain. It was a massive undertaking that ultimately proved unnecessary. The structure was rife with errors. Site work commenced just northeast of Rouses Point, New York, where Lake Champlain empties into the Richelieu River. Military and engineering units were housed at Rouses Point and Champlain. A surveying error discovered that the Americans had broken ground inside Canadian territory. The forty-fifth parallel is the international border, and the American crews were working three quarters of a mile inside Quebec. This brought about the name "Fort Blunder." When the error was discovered, the work was abandoned. Much of the original materials were scavenged by local property owners.

The Webster Ashburton Treaty of 1842 gave the United States the miniscule point of land just north of Rouses Point, and by 1844, construction had resumed. It was named Fort Montgomery after the Revolutionary War general who was in charge of the Quebec invasion in 1776. Construction lasted decades, with heightened activity during the American Civil War. The North had fears Europe would intercede for the South and wanted to prevent an invasion through the Champlain Valley. A detachment infantry was stationed there for several months in 1862. In late 1864, these concerns bore out when almost two dozen Confederates crossed the border from Quebec and raided St. Albans, Vermont. At its peak, the fortress featured walls that were forty-eight feet high, and 125 cannons could be stored there. Although only seventy-five men were ever within its walls, the fort was built to house approximately eight hundred soldiers.

The fort was never really used as a true military installation. Improving technologies rendered stationary bases obsolete. As time turned the page on the 1800s, the fort was effectively abandoned by the U.S. government. In the early 1900s, the location was pillaged by locals for supplies and building materials. During the Great Depression, much of it was demolished and turned into fill for the nearby construction of the Rouses Point Bridge.

The Fort Montgomery Ruins. Significant portions of the fort no longer exist. *Courtesy of Armand Messier, Northern Vermont Aerial Photography.*

A close-up of Fort Montgomery's south wall, one of the few remaining portions of the fort. *Courtesy of Armand Messier, Northern Vermont Aerial Photography.*

Today, Fort Montgomery still partially stands, its south-facing walls a monument to history. Other sections are virtually nonexistent, and remaining portions face structural collapse. Montgomery represents the best and worst of historic preservation in twenty-first-century America. Do the crumbling walls, which were never actually used in combat, represent a critical thread of Lake Champlain history? Do the remaining massive stones, which are still standing but perhaps unsafe, signify an undervalued past? Should the appealing, geometric walls be part of a massive preservation effort? Or should the stones be allowed to crumble and further hide the lake's history?

6

Canal Boats and Steamships

It takes a while for new technology to become common. The first steamship machinery was developed in the late 1790s and early 1800s. The practical use of the steam engine was applied in 1807 and 1808 with the *Vermont*. The boat was built in Burlington and was almost captured by the British during the War of 1812. A second steamer was under construction during that conflict and was purchased by the American naval commander Thomas McDonough.[39] That vessel became the *Ticonderoga* and was badly damaged in the battle of Plattsburgh. The ship was serviceable for a short time afterward but was eventually discarded to rot at the mouth of the Poultney River. The new steam engine technology would make a comeback.

A few different companies dipped their toes into the emerging technology. Between 1815 and 1826, six different steamers were constructed and put into use. The efforts were brand-new, and the kinks were being worked out. There were still a good number of sailing craft on the lake.

The *Phoenix I* was built in Vergennes in 1815 and immediately carried passengers to destinations to the north and south. It was 146 feet long and 27 feet wide. The *Phoenix* was state of the art and boasted many comforts. There were numerous rooms designed for passenger enjoyment, including one for smoking, the passenger cabins, a sitting room, a barbershop, a baggage room and a kitchen.[40]

The next steamer was the *Champlain*, built in 1816 in Vergennes. Originally, it was named the *Vermont*. While traveling the northern regions near the Richelieu River, it became stuck and was critically damaged. The Lake Champlain Steam Company, which owned the *Phoenix*, took on the damaged vessel. After some work, it was relaunched as the *Champlain*. Unfortunately, it was in service for barely a year before it caught fire and burned near Whitehall, New York, in 1817. The next year, the *Congress* was also built at Vergennes. In 1820, the *Phoenix II* was built in the same shipyard. Over the years, the technology was enhanced. A little-known addition to the steamship fleet, the seventy-five-foot-long *General Greene*, was constructed by the Champlain Ferry Company in 1825. It operated exclusively between Port Kent, New York, and Burlington, Vermont.[41]

Another transportation innovation, the Champlain Canal, was finished in the fall of 1823. It was completed at about the same time the main portions of the Eerie Canal, which were about 250 miles long, were finished.[42] Quebec enforced a tariff on lumber originating within the Champlain Valley. Vermont and New York businesses needed the Champlain Canal as an outlet for their timber to reach other markets.[43] This new infrastructure opened a critical waterway which had slowed entire armies in the past. Now, ships from New York City could travel the length of the Hudson River and take the canals through the isolated waters of Lake George. The northern canals opened a direct path to the Richelieu and St. Lawrence Rivers and the markets of Montreal and Quebec City. The larger Erie Canal system allowed goods from Lake Champlain to be sold all the way to the Great Lakes.[44] This was a watershed moment for the area's economic infrastructure and changed the types of craft on the lake. Steamships had been competing with the old-style sailing sloops, but now, canal boats and barges made runs.

Timber, iron ore, crops and marble harvested from the quarries along Lake Champlain suddenly reached other parts of the country.[45] Products were loaded onto sailing ships. They went north through the Richelieu River Canals in Quebec or south toward the Champlain Canal. The time-consuming manual labor of loading and unloading cargo multiple times was very slow.

An entrepreneur from St. Albans designed the first sailing canal boat. It allowed cargo to be loaded and then flow directly into the canal system. The craft needed to navigate only the canal transportation locks. They did not need to be unloaded, reloaded and then unloaded again. This saved time and allowed for fast-moving commerce to explode on Lake Champlain. This was prior to the development of rail travel.

As the decades passed, thousands of different types of canal boats, barges and canal sailing craft moved over Lake Champlain.[46] The lake's traditional merchant sailing ships were just too large to make it through the new docks. The need for smaller canal craft was so large that by 1833, there were 232 cargo- and passenger-carrying canal boats registered with varying lake shore communities. Hundreds more were built. In some cases, they needed to be towed by mules while in the canals.[47]

The year 1827 featured the arrival of the next steamboat ferry, the *Franklin*, built in Saint Albans Bay. It was a significant addition to the burgeoning steamship fleet. It featured refined engine technology, with a seventy-five-horsepower engine, boilers and paddle machinery. The ninety-foot-long *Water Witch*, built at Fort Cassin in 1832, marked the final entry of these early vessels.[48] The *Franklin*, the *Congress* and the new *Phoenix II* moved passengers and freight from the southern reaches to St. Jeans. The economic rivalries brought about cutthroat competition, and there were significant tensions between the different business interests on the lake.[49]

Near the end of those early days, another set of craft emerged: horse ferries. It is not surprising that after wind, paddle and steam, horse-powered craft were attempted. As with the steamers, a specific company invested in and developed them. Henry Ross and Charles McNeil launched horse-powered ferries between Charlotte, Vermont, and Essex, New York. These vessels were the *Eclipse*, the *Gypsy* and the *Eagle*, and they expanded the routes across the lake.[50]

The ferry fleet grew further with the *Winooski*, and the horse-powered *Macdonough*. The firm of Henry Ross and Charles McNeil came to understand that horse ferries could not compete, so they launched the ninety-two-foot-long *Washington*. With so much competition, some of the early entrepreneurs decided to move on from the transportation business. The Lake Champlain Steamboat Company leased its *Phoenix II* and the *Congress* to others who worked mostly with canal boats. The consolidation continued into 1830. The *Phoenix II* wasn't even making passenger runs anymore; it was hauling cargo. The same fate hit the *Washington*, which was effectively used as a tow craft. At one point, there had been more than five competing ferry companies. This number was down to three by the start of the 1830s.

The Champlain Ferry Company, located in Winooski, took over the Burlington–Fort Kent run. It converted the *General Greene* into a more traditional sloop in 1833. By 1835, it was the dominate business interest. It had purchased the *Winooski*, the *Macdonough* and the *Water Witch*. It now owned every steam ferry on Lake Champlain.[51]

The 190-foot-long *Burlington* was built in 1837. She was the most modern steam craft on the lake.[52] The 215-foot-long steamship *Whitehall* was purchased from a rival interest and launched in 1837. Charles Dickens, while visiting the United States in 1842, was ferried by the *Burlington*. He described the vessel as "a perfectly exquisite achievement of neatness, elegance, and order." That same year, the Champlain Steamboat Company replaced the older *Winooski* with the newer *Saranac*. Business interests in New York began to criticize the near monopoly on Lake Champlain. Steps were taken to ensure competition, with the New York legislature approving the new (but similarly named) Champlain Steam Transportation Company. In a move worthy of the coming robber barons, the Champlain Steamboat Company simply bought out the investors for its new rival and avoided major competition. However, in 1844, Peter Comstock built the 185-foot-long *Francis Saltus*, which served as direct competition to the *Burlington*. Comstock was able to compete for a short while, but soon, he sold his financial investment to outside interests. The competition created a bidding war for customers, and travelers benefited.

Meanwhile, the canal boat economy continued to grow. The operators were extremely busy, and in some cases, the boats served as homes for them. Some even had their families living on board with them. Examining all the canal boats on the lake would be an impossible task. However, there are glimpses that provide a lens into what was happing at the time. In the 1840s, three of the active canal boats were the *Middlebury*, the *J. Sherman* and the *Garland*. They transported travelers west to other parts of the new canal system.[53] To tackle the time issues from moving so much cargo, the Burlington-based Merchants Lake Boat Line designed new canal sailing craft in 1841. These state-of-the-art boats were very desirable, as they moved through the canals very easily. After 1842, the ship building of traditional sailing vessels experienced a huge decline. The addition of these new vessels even made the use of tugs obsolete.[54] When the new sailing barges were deployed, they could take down their mast and rigging.[55]

Farther north, larger boat traffic was finally able to go through the Richelieu River and the Chambly Canal after 1843. The Quebec government wanted to take advantage of the commerce on Lake Champlain, and it made sure the Chambly Canal was opened.[56] Prior to this, the loading and unloading of cargo had consumed painstaking amounts of time. Now, markets in the Great Lakes were accessed very easily.[57] Even farmers took advantage of this transportation venue, using the canal system to move apples, butter, cheese, grain, potatoes and other products to cities on the eastern seaboard.

The steamship *Macdonough* was on the lake for a little more than a decade. It sank off Panton Bay, west of Addison County, Vermont. Interests organized to compete with the Champlain Transportation Company. The *United States* was launched in 1847. It was a 240-foot-long steamer and was easily the most advanced ship on the lake. It traveled an impressive nineteen miles an hour and featured comfortable rooms for passengers. By the end of the 1840s the Champlain Transportation Company was picking off the competition again, as it acquired the *Francis Saltus*. It also purchased the *Montreal*, another ship that was being constructed by a potential rival.

There were other steamers, but they were not passenger vessels. Companies had interest in freight traffic, and a number of craft were deployed for this purpose. While canal barges made their way north and south, the freight steamships were the *James H. Hooker*, the *Ethan Allen*, *Boquet*, *Boston* and the *Oliver Bascom*.

Railroads snaked through the Champlain Valley, and their financial tendrils spread into Lake Champlain. By the 1850s, rail companies had purchased a few of the lake's freight steamers, which complemented their ability to move cargo quickly through the Champlain Valley.[58]

More competition emerged against the Champlain Transportation Company. T.D. Chapman and Associates launched the 250-foot-long steamer, the *R.W. Sherman*, in 1852. The influence of rail played out, and the Champlain Transportation Company sold all of its assets to the Rutland and Burlington Railroad that year. In a twist of irony, it purchased the freshly launched *R.W. Sherman* and 260-foot-long *Canada*, the new steamer that was being finished in Whitehall. It was a brilliant economic move, as the company kept its charter, sold off its older vessels and obtained the two newest steamers on Lake Champlain. The rail companies soon understood how difficult the steamship business was and, just two years later, in 1854, washed their hands of the old craft they had just acquired. The aged steamers *Burlington*, *United States*, *Whitehall* and *Saranac* once again fell into the hands of the Champlain Transportation Company for just one-third of their original sale price.

Pure capitalism brought about the end of many vessels. Due to age and repair issues, the *Burlington*, *Saranac* and *Whitehall* were sent to Shelburne Harbor and partially dismantled. The *United States*, *Canada* and *America* continued their service. The *Francis Saltus* was the subject of a few tense transactions, one of which degenerated into a confrontation at gunpoint. Eventually, that vessel was also brought to Shelburne Bay, where it became a member of the discarded fleet already there. Around this time, the *Montreal* was reacquired by the Lake Champlain Transportation Company.

The growth in water transport impacted local economies significantly. A perfect example is the story of the Burleigh brothers, whose influence and entrepreneurship brought considerable growth to southern Lake Champlain. They realized the profit potential of transporting goods by sailing canal boat, and in 1859, they created the firm of Burleighs and Marshall. The next year, they began building their fleet of canal boats. Eventually, the company owned approximately 150 canal boats and steamers. They carried lumber, iron ore and coal to and from Canadian markets to the Great Lakes and eastern seaboard.[59] The firm owned the Smith Mine in Port Henry, New York.

The boat-building frenzy reached smaller, more isolated communities. The team of Moore and Holye created wharves along a section of the Great Chazy River. It empties into the lake just south of Rouses Point, New York. Kellogg and Averill's boatyard soon followed, and by 1879, a third boat-building facility was constructed on the river. By 1862, twenty million feet of lumber had been cut and sailed down the Chazy River. This wood was used for homes in other parts of the country and fueled the steam engines on Lake Champlain.[60]

An example of how much the lake was woven into the regional economy was industry's need for iron ore. By 1860, the mines in New York produced 20 percent of the country's iron, which was consumed at ravenous rates during the Civil War. This brought much prosperity to the eastern Adirondacks.[61]

By mid-century, one of the most prominent shipyards was located in Essex, New York. Scores of sailing canal boats were built there. The *General Butler* was built there in 1862. In three years, it earned so much profit, its owners simply sold it to someone else. It served its purpose, and other parties wanted in on the action.[62]

In 1867, the 251-foot-long *Adirondack* was built. It marked the transition from wood- to coal-powered steamers. In 1868, the *Montreal*'s time as a passenger ship ended. It was converted to primarily towing duties. Smaller ferrying operations commenced. The Saint Albans, Grand Isle and Plattsburgh Ferry Company operated the *River Queen*. It ran regular routes between St. Albans Bay, Maquam Bay and Plattsburgh. Its time was short-lived, as it hit rocks around Hathaway Point and sank in October 1868. The small *Grand Isle* operated out of Essex, New York, but was later sold to rail interests. In the early 1870s, the steamer *A. Williams* operated out of Burlington, built by a smaller company. It ended up in the hands of the Lake Champlain Transportation Company and had a productive two-decade career. One of the newest and most powerful freight steamers was the *L.J.N Stark*, but it had one of the shortest hauling careers. It was built in 1869 but sank off Point au Roche, just north of Plattsburgh, in 1870. The use of canal barges likely peaked in the 1870s.[63]

In 1871, the 262-foot-long *Vermont II* was built next. It was the most impressive craft on the lake, with sixty-one staterooms, a presidential room, a bridal room, a barbershop and a 150-foot-long dining room. It represented the best efforts to comfort passengers on Lake Champlain. It reached speeds of nineteen miles per hour and was a very attractive vessel.

In 1873, the impressive *Oak Ames* operated on the lake and was owned by the CTC. In 1875, its name was changed to the *Champlain*, but it sank just north of Ticonderoga.

By 1875, the *Adirondack* suffered from incurable engine and hull vibrations, and it was taken out of service. The competition from rail transport probably made the decision a little easier. That year, the railroad line from Ticonderoga to Plattsburgh was completed. Rail now ran north and south on both sides of the lake. The steam ferries were still effective transport, but the industry was in the same position as the dinosaurs. The *Adirondack* was taken to Shelburne Bay. Eventually, it sank near Colamers Island in about fifteen feet of water.

Another example of the maritime traffic's positive impact on local economies occurred when the Burleigh brothers began constructing canal boats just south of Laribee's Point in Vermont. This was near the Addison County railroad bridge. A sawmill was erected that used the lumber from the region to produce boards. That wood was immediately used to construct canal boats. In a three-year period between 1879 and 1881, the Burleighs built several of their one-hundred-ton canal boats.[64]

The steamship *Maquam* in Maquam Bay. *Courtesy of the Swanton Historical Society.*

The steamship *Chateaugay* proudly chugging along on Lake Champlain. *Library of Congress, public domain.*

The aged steamer *Montreal*, relegated to towing duties for the previous twelve years, burned in Maquam Bay in 1880.[65] Ironically, the steamer *Maquam* was built in Swanton that same year. It was constructed to take advantage of the rail lines, offering a mixed transportation experience of rail and water. One of the few steamships not owned by the Lake Champlain Transportation Company was the *Reindeer*, completed in 1881. It was built in Alburgh and was operated by the Grand Isle Steamship Company.[66]

The Delaware and Hudson Railroad looked to improve steamboat travel. It constructed the 205-foot-long *Chateauguay* in 1888. It was the first of the steamers to totally abandon the commonplace wooden frame and was constructed using iron.

In the 1890s, the *A. Williams* was brought into Shelburne Bay and discarded, adding to the growing list of steamers collecting at the bottom of the lake. In 1897, the *Maquam* was purchased by the CTC for runs between Burlington and St. Albans.

The arrival of trains eventually put the canal barges and boats out of business, but the decline took several decades. There were upgrades to different parts of the canal system in the early 1900s, but moving freight by rail was timelier and more cost effective.[67]

By the end of the nineteenth century, much of Vermont's forestland had been harvested, and the area was importing Canadian lumber. By 1908, one register documented that forty-three sail barges, twenty-five canal boats and fourteen barges had come south, full of lumber. The year before, there had been 148 boatloads of lumber from Canada.[68]

In 1902, the *Reindeer* was disassembled. The Delaware and Hudson Railroad constructed the *Vermont III* in 1903 and the *Ticonderoga* in 1906.[69] The *Vermont III* was huge, measuring 262 feet long and 62 feet wide. Some described it as a floating palace, as it had individual rooms with running water, a lavish staircase and an enormous stateroom. These years brought on the retirement of the *Maquam*, which had served on the lake for twenty-four years. At the end of its time, in 1904, it became yet another steamer brought to Shelburne Bay.[70]

The *Chateaugay* ran passenger service up until 1924. Its still-solid frame was reconstructed and redesigned, and it became the first vessel to cater to automobile traffic going east-west between Vermont and New York. The Great Depression and World War II brought the virtual end to the steamer era on Lake Champlain. Additionally, the advent of the personal automobile

The steamship *Vermont*. *Library of Congress, public domain.*

The steamship *Ticonderoga* sailing along the broad lake. *Library of Congress, public domain.*

A group of canal boats on Lake Champlain. *Courtesy of the Swanton Historical Society.*

spelled the end of mass transit over the lake. In the early years of World War II, the *Ticonderoga*, *Vermont III* and the *Chateaugay* made only occasional runs. In the 1940s, the *Chateauguay* was removed from service. What was left of its hull was dismantled and transported out of the area.

In 1963, the *Ticonderoga* was preserved and moved to the Shelburne Museum. It is one of the main attractions and allows visitors to see what an original steamship looked like.

7

Trains over the Lake

R ail connected cities and helped define early industrialization in the United States. The story sometimes involved large bodies of water that needed to be dealt with. The tale of how rail moved over water is truly unique.

Early tracks connected cities in the 1830s and 1840s. Vermont got into the action a few years later. Rail moved in from the south and crept toward northern Vermont at a slow crawl. As the original lines moved west, there were questions about how to link Boston and New York with Montreal in Quebec. Soon, rail linked Burlington and Essex to St. Albans, and investors looked for the best way to bridge Lake Champlain.

There was no easy solution. Competing train companies proposed different routes over the forty-fifth parallel. There was the question of private landowners, who had legitimate interests measured against economic growth. Finally, there was the lake's steamships, which didn't want to lose out to the infant railroad industry. When the dust settled, lines went over small rivers, bays and waterways and connected the shores of Quebec, New York and Vermont.

Northern Vermont was not geographically easy to deal with. To the northwest was the unique town of Alburgh, a peninsula jutting down from Canada. This land feature necessitated that two separate bridges be built: one from New York, just south of the Canadian line, and another to stretch from Alburgh's eastern shore to Vermont. When it was completed, Upstate New York and Quebec would be linked to some of America's largest cities.

As early as March 1850, one of the first concepts was developed.[71] The connecting tracks and infrastructure needed to run north through several western Vermont towns. The foreshadowing of something larger came when the work over the Lamoille River was underway in the final weeks of August.[72] In New York, after October 1, customers could go from Ogdensburg, New York, and points along the St. Lawrence River to Rouses Point.[73] Soon, the piers for the bridge going over Missisquoi Bay were nearly finished. This was an accomplishment, but it was not the only objective.

By October, the plan moved from concept to reality. The project needed a rubber stamp of approval from the Vermont legislature, and Governor Paine wanted the movers and shakers to see the progress firsthand.

In the days leading up to Halloween, members of the general assembly gathered with the governor in St. Albans. The public was invited to join the "north-western expedition." As various groups arrived, they were brought to the hotels of St. Albans. They enjoyed coffee and rolls from Cole's Pavilion, Barber's United States Hotel and Danforth's Hotel. After socializing, carriages brought the nearly three hundred observers down to St. Albans Bay, where the steamer *Ethan Allen* waited.[74]

The ship left the docks and moved north toward Missisquoi Bay. The journey was like a tourist expedition. Scattered showers brought periodic rain, with rolling, wispy clouds curling over the Champlain Islands. The post-peak foliage still dotted the landscape. As the steamboat chugged north, observers noticed something on the northern horizon.

Something was growing in the distant water.

The curious onlookers gathered on the deck of the *Ethan Allen*. Along the horizon, west of Swanton's Hog Island, a mass was on the waterline. The boat moved beyond the edge of North Hero. To the west, Alburgh's coast came into view. There, something snaked across the water.

Shorter distances provide clarity.

Some called it a "sea serpent" others called it the "thousand-legged monster." The legislators and dignitaries observed northern Vermont being connected to the rest of the world. It wasn't quite done, but they witnessed history in the making. Dozens and dozens of workmen, engineers and railroad employees hammered away at the link between West Swanton and Alburgh. The *Ethan Allen* entered Missisquoi Bay and came back. It repeated the maneuver, giving everyone ample opportunity to see rail lines being set. Thirty-six piers were in place, each lifting the tracks twelve feet above the water. The sections were thirty feet long, all supported by

What remains of the train bridge connecting Rouses Point, New York, to Alburgh, Vermont. *Courtesy of Armand Messier, Northern Vermont Aerial Photography.*

six wooden pylons submerged to the lake bottom. The seventy-foot-long drawbridge was under construction.

The steamer moved south, hugging the Alburgh coast. It rounded the peninsula's southern tip and approached Rouses Point. There, they spied America's Fort Montgomery resting on the Canadian Border. In the distance was the custom house that had regulated trade with Canada for decades. To the north and west, they saw more unique the engineering work. At Rouses Point, the Ogdensburg Railroad was preparing the bridge to connect with Alburgh's Windmill Point. The steamer returned to St. Albans, the invited guests having witnessed history in the making.

While the rail line was impressive and new, the work was controversial. Those who owned the canal boats and steamers knew what the coming of rail meant. Freight would move more quickly over land, making their ships undesirable. These interests were part of the safety discussion about the size of the rail bridges on both sides of Alburgh.[75] Many of these concerns were brushed aside, interpreted as the boat owners wanting to protect their interests.

A close-up view of what remains of the former Rouses Point train bridge. *Courtesy of Armand Messier, Northern Vermont Aerial Photography.*

On the Vermont side, the work was not easy. It involved creating a trestle bridge over a span of 4,200 feet. Much of it was done by an army of men who had worked on rail in other states. By early December, the Missisquoi Bay section was completed.[76] Seven miles across Alburgh, the engineers labored furiously against the descending cold, getting in the final lengths prior to the ice freezing. The connection between Windmill Point and Rouses Point was almost done. At this point, everyone could see the coming benefits of rail. In spring, summer and most of the fall, the steamships had no problem sailing the lake. With the final weeks of December at hand, only two vessels, the *Saranac* and the *Ethan Allen*, still operated.[77] With the approaching ice, that number dwindled to zero.

By the end of the second week of January 1851, Alburgh was linked on both sides. It was an upgrade to transportation that changed the travel economy in the Northeast. When rail finally linked Rouses Point to Alburgh and then Swanton, someone could travel from Boston to points farther west in two days.[78] It was a watershed change, and passengers and freight immediately moved through the area.[79]

Trains being able to travel over Lake Champlain was an engineering marvel. *Courtesy of the Swanton Historical Society.*

While the bridges were impressive, sometimes accidents did happen. *Courtesy of the Swanton Historical Society.*

The lake was again bridged later on, although it was a much smaller project. Economic progress brings innovation and competition, and some wondered if another east-west line would benefit the state's infrastructure. Work began on the Addison Railroad, which would run from preexisting rail near the Vermont towns of Leicester and Brandon in Addison County to Lake Champlain. These tracks would then go over water to Ticonderoga, New York, with the new terminus being a hub between New York City and Plattsburgh.[80] The project required sixteen miles of new track to be put down through several small Vermont communities. By November 1869, some of the first work had been completed. It extended west through Whiting, hit the southeast corner of Shoreham and then the northeastern shoulder of Orwell. The plan was to have the bridge work occur just south of Larabee's Point in Shoreham.[81] These proposals were not set in stone as late as January 1870.[82] The project was seen as economic progress for central portions of the state. Towns like Middlebury and Bridport wondered how they might benefit.[83] The land route became secondary, as questions about the location of the bridge continued. By October 1870, everything was finally in place. H.W. and J.W. Phelps out of Springfield, Massachusetts, was contracted for the work. It brought in another firm, Hawkins, Herthal and Burrall's Ironworks, to build the nearly half-mile-long structure.[84] Ground was broken, and the work commenced in Whiting on Saturday, November 5.[85] The railroad directors promoted a completion date for the next summer. Delays unfolded; months passed.

American history is full of stories that involved dangerous railroad work, and the story of this bridge was no different. On Thursday, January 26, 1871, local papers described a horrible accident. Close to the lake, the frozen ground gave way. Thirteen workers experienced a cave-in. Eleven men emerged; two had been buried alive.[86] One was an Englishman, Dan McGinnis, the other was Irishmen, Christopher Conners.

The work on the New York side still needed to be ironed out.[87] Considerable opposition emerged in the towns of Whitehall and Troy. At stake were the lumber and iron interests in Upstate New York, which wanted another north-south line. As the calendar moved into February, company construction plans were released to the press.[88] The design called for a nearly three-hundred-foot-long swinging drawbridge to prevent obstructing boat traffic. The structure was to be supported by timber cribs that were filled with stone and sunk one hundred feet apart. By early March, the first work had started.[89]

There was another mishap in Vermont. The project had reached Shoreham, but another worker was killed when frozen earth once again gave way.[90] The press described the man as a Frenchman, Fredrick Bouttant.

April brought warmer weather and more attention to the project. The companies advertised that they needed about five hundred men to work on the Addison County Railroad. Their wages would be $1.75 per day.[91] With so many workers, accidents were not the only problems. In early May, there was concern that some of the laborers were showing up to work drunk.[92] One was arrested and jailed for the sin of public drunkenness.[93]

Most of the work on the 1,800-foot-long trestle bridge started in June and continued through the summer. At least fifty men worked on the structure each day.[94]

The bridge was completed by the fall, but there were already problems.[95] Newspaper accounts reported that high winds and strong storms had caused damage. It had been in operation for only a few weeks. Despite the early damage, the first train embarked over it in December 1871.

The final large rail bridge project occurred near the end of the nineteenth century. The Rutland Canadian Railway proposed connecting Burlington to Grand Isle County. The line would traverse the Lake Champlain Islands and connect with the larger yards in Alburgh and Rouses Point. This line would begin construction in 1899. Once the charter was approved by the Vermont legislature, the company wasted no time. By January that year, it explored different proposals. If built, it would shave sixteen miles off the existing route from Burlington to Swanton and Rouses Point.[96]

The initial tracks were laid along King Street in Burlington. By February, the Rutland and Canada executive board received bid offers. The plans had small drawbridges between Colchester Point and South Hero, another between South Hero and North Hero and a final one connecting North Hero and Alburgh. The company committed to a railroad station in each town in Grand Isle County.[97] As the weather warmed, rumors swirled about behind-the-scenes, industrial big-money players. The Vanderbilts had interests in Upstate New York rail. Speculation rose that the Rutland and Canadian project might establish a franchised line from Boston to the Great Lakes.[98]

On March 2, the company went public with very specific plans. Doing the work was O'Brien and Sheehan out of New York City, who had arranged for the heavy equipment to arrive in Plattsburgh during the winter. After March 9, the contractors set about improving the grades of certain plots of land; 12 steam drills, 6 hoisting machines, 4 boilers, about 150 dumping cars and 5,000 railroad ties were impressively brought over the winter ice. When the ice melted, at least 4 locomotive engines and 3 steam shovels were ferried across. As temperatures hovered around freezing, nearly three hundred workers were already in use. Two hundred more had already started near Trump's Point in northern Grand Isle. The rock and stone that would serve as the foundation for the bridges was harvested in Colchester. Similarly, in South Hero, thousands of yards of stone were cut. Preparations were made for another two thousand workers to arrive. Management wanted the entire line from Burlington up to Rouses Point completed by October.[99] With the work underway, officials shared the potential routes. The Colchester–Grand Isle causeway bridge would be over three miles long. The line would run northwest of Keeler Bay and then up to Grand Isle Village. A half-mile bridge and drawbridge would connect Bow's Point to Arrow Point in southern North Hero. It would hug the western shore all the way to Pellot's Point, and then a third bridge would connect to Alburgh. It would run to the already existing line in town.

There were right-of-way issues. By mid-April, representatives had communicated with the affected landowners, and the access issues were being worked out.[100] As summer approached, a few more right-of-way and payment issues cropped up. While the railroad sought to purchase land in North Hero, some landowners had issues with the Rutland and Canadian Railroad.

Another fatality occurred in May, when a worker was feared to have drowned. He was the night watchman at Allen's Point and was seen during his regular shift. The next morning, he was just gone.[101]

In early June, Grand Isle resident Stephen Hoag furnished a large amount of the timber for the project.[102] Then there was a strike of railroad workers. Management announced plans to bring in 150 Italians to replace them. The infrastructure was soon in place for the rock to be harvested in the islands and brought between Colchester Point and the southern areas of South Hero. It was almost shallow enough to walk across there. Soon, only two hundred feet of the causeway needed to be filled in.[103] Two locomotive engines and nearly thirty railcars hauled large stones from South Hero to the lake. Steam drills, steam shovels and pile drivers were in use a mile from Keeler's Bay. Heavy equipment worked near Trump's Point and Pellot's Point. Nearly 450 railroad men worked on the island, two-thirds of them Italians. Soon, 200 men were connecting the line to Colchester Point.

Men from all over the country were brought in to get the work done. In late July, a team of more than ninety-five "Negro" laborers arrived in the Burlington area.[104] Summer turned to fall, and the original timetable for completion was abandoned. If the weather wasn't too severe, it was hoped the laborers could stay working throughout the winter.[105] In late October, a man's leg was crushed while he was hauling stone for the bridge supports out of Grand Isle.[106] It was not easy work. In some cases, laborers were in such dire situations that they robbed other workers. In November, a man working in Grand Isle was robbed of about seventy dollars.[107]

Not everyone liked the presence of so many foreign workmen. In Burlington's North Avenue region, a man was sick and tired of employees from the Rutland and Canada walking across his property at night. He started guarding his land with a shotgun.[108]

As late as November 17, dynamite was still being used to blast the path of the railroad.[109]

A month later, another accident occurred. A train bumped the cars on the new trestle bridge, and they fell off and sank. Eight railcars lay in about thirty feet of water twelve miles south of St. Albans.[110] Other deadly accidents still occurred. Late in December, near North Hero, one of the brakemen fell onto the tracks. The train was moving, and the wheels severed his head from the rest of his body.[111] On December 23, there were still nearly nine hundred workers hammering away.[112]

The end of the year featured a surprise, a mini "railroad war." The tension was over who would have the rights to the repaired bridge from Rouses Point to Windmill Point. The Rutland and Canadian was nearly finished, but other railroad companies didn't mind if the new line experienced problems. The employees of the Central Vermont Railway, which was the existing line from Burlington, Swanton and over to Alburgh, attempted to take over the operation of the Windmill Point bridge. The effort failed, and both companies attained access to the single bridge.[113]

The effort dragged on. In January 1900, the link between Grand Isle and North Hero was still under construction.[114] Despite the frigid conditions and the men getting sick with scarlet fever, the labor continued.[115] More Italian immigrants were brought in from Boston to complete the project.[116] Weeks later, the connection between Colchester and South Hero was almost complete. The new fill brought the tracks approximately twelve feet above the lake. The construction was dangerous, and one of the pile drivers fell into the lake at one point.[117] The Italian workers continued to make the press. In late February, one worker stabbed another in the neck with a knife.[118] Chittenden County authorities responded. The wounded man was given medical attention, and the assailant was nowhere to be found. In early March, some of the Italians just left their jobs, perhaps sick of the winter conditions.[119] The accidents continued into the spring. In one case, a Mr. Blackwood, an engineer who was toiling in Grand Isle, had a railroad spike go through his lips.[120]

The final engineering projects, the bridges, received the most attention at the end.[121] The workers were still exposed to risky conditions. Blasting continued for causeway fill. During the explosions, it was typical for workers to lay in hiding behind trees or bluffs. One man emerged from his concealment too early. Rocks flew as though they were fired from a cannon. One rock hit him in the leg, which was instantly shattered.[122]

And it happened again. In early June, two men, George Miner of Swanton and Jerry McNally, were injured during another blasting session. Pieces of stone were launched across the work zone. Miner survived the incident but was listed as delirious. McNally, whose body was shredded, his head was struck by the projectiles, did not survive.[123]

Trains still chug over Lake Champlain today, but their routes are limited. The story of these mechanical beasts roaring along is, for the most part, obscured by the past.

8

Grand Hotels and Resorts of Lake Champlain

In the nineteenth century, as steam and rail transportation made travel easier and more affordable for the middle class, tourism became a booming industry. America's cities were growing rapidly, and it became desirable and fashionable to spend the hot summer months in the mountains, where the air was cooler and cleaner and perceived to be healthful. Lake Champlain was a major attraction, and the Adirondacks were a particularly popular destination. The tourist trade was eagerly embraced by many New York and Vermont communities, especially those whose population had begun to stagnate due to migration to the Midwest and beyond. The State of New York created the Adirondack Park in 1892, and its hotels, attractions and natural splendors were heavily promoted in city newspapers. At six million acres, the Adirondack Park is the largest park in the United States.

Westport Inn: Westport, New York

The Westport Inn was a highly popular tourist destination for ninety years. Located on the shores of Lake Champlain and considered the gateway to the Adirondack Mountains, Westport benefited from the nineteenth century's great progress in transportation. The opening of the Champlain Canal in 1823, the development of steamship travel and the arrival of the Delaware and Hudson Railroad line in 1876 made this small hamlet a

Lake Champlain was a destination for vacationers. The popular Westport Inn attracted a lot of business. *Library of Congress, public domain.*

hub of activity. Westport had a large commercial dock and was the home dock for the *Ticonderoga* steamboat in the early twentieth century.[124] The town had several attractions, including the county fairgrounds, children's summer camps and medicinal springs that attracted travelers seeking a healthful retreat in the country.

The Westport Inn began business in 1877, developed on the site of a former lakeside tavern. Eventually a sprawling resort, the three-story inn was known for its beautiful gardens, well-maintained beach and lovely views of the lake and Green Mountains. As sports became increasingly popular, a putting green, a croquet lawn and tennis courts were added. Boating and fishing expeditions were organized for guests, and the inn was also a convenient homebase for day trips by ferry to other sites on the lake. A bar and grill offered live music and dancing in the 1940s and 1950s. In 1967, the Westport Inn was demolished. The site's owner subsequently donated the land to the Town of Westport for the creation of a town park.[125]

MISSISQUOI SPRINGS HOTEL: SHELDON, VERMONT

The Missisquoi Springs Hotel was one of eleven hotels and boardinghouses that were built in the town of Sheldon to provide lodging during a tourist boom from 1865 to 1870. The sudden influx of visitors came to experience the reputed health benefits of Sheldon's six mineral springs. Mineral springs and spas were something of a health fad during the post–Civil War era, with many grand claims about the miraculous healing effects of mineral water from pure mountain springs. A county history published in 1891 reported, "The water from the Missisquoi spring in particular is bottled and sent to all parts of the country. The specialty claimed for the water of this spring is a remedy for cancer, scrofula, and other diseases of the skin and blood."[126] Sheldon is considered by some to have been the leading mineral waters resort of the era.

The Missisquoi Springs Hotel was built by C. Bainbridge Smith, a Manhattan attorney who claimed that the mineral springs in town had cured his tongue cancer. Mr. Smith became such an enthusiast of the mineral springs that he purchased the Missisquoi Spring in 1865; he began bottling and shipping the water and built the hotel in 1867. The Missisquoi Springs

The Missisquoi Springs Hotel in Sheldon, Vermont. The train and steamship economy allowed even the small towns to attract out-of-state travelers. *Courtesy of the Sheldon Historical Society.*

Hotel had one hundred rooms and was "finished and furnished in the style of first class city hotels. Water and gas are carried to every room." Smith intended to add additional wings to his hotel, but unfortunately, it burned down in 1870.[127]

Hotel Ausable Chasm: Keeseville, New York

Built near the awe-inspiring and beautiful Ausable Chasm, this Adirondack hotel was accessible to travelers by rail. Ausable Chasm, a sandstone gorge often touted as the "Grand Canyon of the Adirondacks," opened to the public in 1870, spurring the growth of services such as tours, lodging and dining for summer visitors. The hotel was built in 1897 and accommodated approximately two hundred guests. Poised on a bluff overlooking the chasm's famous Rainbow Falls, with views of Lake Champlain, the Adirondacks and

The Hotel Ausable Chasm was a very attractive destination in Upstate New York. *Library of Congress, public domain.*

the Green Mountains, it was a luxurious resort that was four stories high with a large wrap-around porch. It boasted an artesian well and a modern elevator.[128] With its grand views, the hotel hosted events such as the banquet for the 1922 graduating class of the University of Vermont and a Mason's convention that hosted U.S. Supreme Court justice Arthur S. Tompkins.[129] During the 1920s, the hotel offered dancing accompanied by a full orchestra. The Hotel Ausable Chasm burned down in 1950.

HOTEL MAQUAM: SWANTON, VERMONT

The Hotel Maquam, sometimes known as Hotel Champlain, was situated on a twenty-five-acre park on Maquam Shore, south of Missisquoi Bay. In 1876, the three-story hotel was moved to Maquam Shore from the town of Sheldon, where it had been built and operated as the Bellevue House. Operating only during the summer season, it could accommodate ninety patrons.[130] In its early years, the steamer *Maquam* often transported guests to the hotel. Steamships sailing the calm waters of the northern lake would bring passengers to shore, where they could disembark and enjoy the hotel's

Hotel Champlain at Maquam benefited from being located right on the lake. Steamships could drop vacationers off directly in front of the hotel, and a train line could bring them right into Swanton. *Courtesy of the Swanton Historical Society.*

grounds or connect with a small rail link that ran into to the village of Swanton, providing quick access to any happenings in town.[131] The location was a transportation link between Lake Champlain and other communities in northwest Vermont, with a quick train ride between Swanton and the St. Albans rail hub.

Fishing in the bay was a prime attraction, with small mouth bass, muskie and pike all plentiful. Small boats for sailing the waters of Northern Lake Champlain were available from the hotel. The hotel's outdoor games included tennis, baseball, croquet and golf. Its indoor recreation activities included bowling, pool tables and shuffleboard. Three music concerts were provided daily.[132] The Hotel Maquam burned down in 1920.

ISLAND VILLA HOTEL: GRAND ISLE, VERMONT

Thoughtfully preserved in 1998 by the Preservation Trust of Vermont, this charming hotel still exists as the Grand Isle Lake House, a conference and event center. Built in 1903, the original inn was known as the Island Villa

The Lake House in Grand Isle had the benefit of being surrounded by Lake Champlain. *Library of Congress, public domain.*

Hotel. Although it was not as large as many resorts of the time, Island Villa had electricity and running water, uncommon amenities in a rural area at that time and ones that certainly appealed to wealthy city people looking to escape the summer heat. The hotel's success relied in part on the new Rutland and Canadian Railroad line, which opened in 1900, connecting the Champlain Islands with the major cities of the eastern seaboard.

Island Villa had extensive flower and vegetable gardens that supplied produce for the hotel's kitchen, and its eggs and cream came from the farm next door. Fishing, boating and swimming were available, along with tennis, croquet, ping pong and shuffleboard. The Island Villa operated until 1956, when it was purchased by the Sisters of Mercy and operated as a girls' summer camp until the early 1990s.[133]

Missisquoi Park: Highgate Springs, Vermont

Missisquoi Park was a lakeside park created in 1880 by Central Vermont Railway as a summer destination that would appeal to rail passengers.[134] Located on Missisquoi Bay, close to the Canadian border, the park was adjacent to the new rail line, making it an ideal spot for developing the type of scenic recreation that was becoming increasingly popular with the middle-class public. Missisquoi Park became a common destination for day trips, where families could enjoy outdoor activities, such as fishing, swimming, croquet and picnicking. Lodgings, boat rental companies, a telegraph station and an ice cream stand sprung up nearby to serve visitors, and a pavilion for gatherings was added. Walking trails and foot bridges graced the property. Small skiffs gave people the chance to row out and enjoy the view from Rock Island, commonly called Bandstand Island today.[135] Henry Ward Beecher, a famous abolitionist and social reformer, gave a lecture at Missisquoi Park in July 1880.[136] Today, the park property still welcomes summer visitors as part of the Tyler Place Family Resort.

The Windsor: Elizabethtown, New York

The Windsor was an expansive summer hotel built in the 1880s by Orlando Kellogg, a member of a prominent Elizabethtown family. Kellogg's 1929

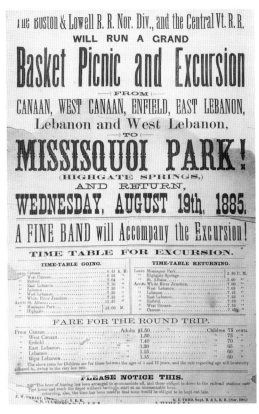

The Boston & Lowell R. R. Nor. Div., and the Central Vt. R. R.

WILL RUN A GRAND

Basket Picnic and Excursion

— FROM —

CANAAN, WEST CANAAN, ENFIELD, EAST LEBANON, Lebanon and West Lebanon,

— TO —

MISSISQUOI PARK!

(HIGHGATE SPRINGS,)

AND RETURN,

WEDNESDAY, AUGUST 19th, 1885.

A FINE BAND will Accompany the Excursion!

TIME TABLE FOR EXCURSION.

Left: Missisquoi Park was a destination that was tucked into the extreme northwest corner of Vermont. *Courtesy of the Highgate Historical Society.*

Below: The isolated waters of Missisquoi Bay provided a wonderful vacation spot for weary travelers. *Courtesy of the Highgate Historical Society.*

Upstate New York provided plenty of places to get away. The hotel in Elizabethtown, New York, was quite popular. *Public domain.*

obituary states that he served in Washington, D.C., during the Civil War; was "well acquainted" with Abraham Lincoln; and was part of the honor guard that kept watch over abolitionist John Brown's coffin on its journey home for burial near Lake Placid.[137] In the late nineteenth century, Elizabethtown's beauty and location made it one of the most prominent resort communities in the Adirondacks. As the Windsor was located only a few miles from Westport, tourists could arrive by steamer or train and be picked up at the Westport dock or station by Orland Kellogg's stagecoach service.

The hotel was built in an L shape; it was three stories tall with wrap-around porches on the first and second floors. On top of the building were four large cupolas, with windows overlooking the mountains. In its heyday, the Windsor had 150 rooms, many with private baths. A 1916 advertisement in the *Brooklyn Daily Eagle* promoted the hotel as newly redecorated. "The Windsor is the embodiment of everything modern in hotel equipment, with that homelike air of refinement and comfort so much desired by families summering in the mountains....Golf, Tennis, Hunting, Fishing, Riding, Driving, Dancing, Automobiling, and a diversity of social functions furnish interesting entertainment during the season."[138] After eighty years of serving Adirondack hospitality, the Windsor was razed in 1968.[139]

9

THE WORD OF GOD

The Millerites

And I looked, and behold a pale horse: and his name that sat on him was Death,
and Hell followed with him.
Revelations 6:8

One of the most intriguing episodes in the history of the Champlain Valley occurred when William Miller predicted the end of the world. The holy man, who lived and ministered very close to the lake's shore, calculated when the second coming of Christ would occur. For more than a decade, believers were convinced the end of days would come at some point during the 1840s. When the much-anticipated date approached, Miller and his followers organized to observe how the book Revelations might play out. They didn't undertake a pilgrimage to the holy land. They did not set off for some ancient church. The prophet and his followers waited for the world to end near the southern tip of Lake Champlain.

Religious men have been interpreting the Old and New Testaments for ages. According to religious belief, the son of God is supposed to return to Earth. The final pages of the Bible provide details. Believers are to be saved, and a new kingdom of Christianity will arise. Nonbelievers, sinners and deniers of Jesus as their savior are to be cast into internal damnation.

One might ponder if such events would unfold in the Middle East. It is the birthplace of three major world religions. It is where Mosses parted the Red Sea.

William Miller was born in Pittsfield, Massachusetts, in 1782. He was raised in an era when religion was a major influence in people's lives. Few were literate, and everyday life was a matter of survival. Reading was a luxury. The Bible was one of the few books that was readily available. Holy men understood the power of faith, especially among a population that was not well educated. Interpreting the Bible allowed a privileged few to hold sway over large segments of the population. In the late 1790s, when Miller was a child, the founding fathers were honoring the promises of the U.S. Constitution. The fledgling American republic was to be run by the people, not a king or pope.

Thomas Paine, one of the most published writers of the era, wrote in 1794, "Whenever we read the obscene stories, the voluptuous debaucheries, the cruel and tortuous executions, the unrelenting vindictiveness, with which more than half of the Bible is filled, it would be more consistent that we called it a work of a demon, than the word of God. It is a history of wickedness, that has served to corrupt and brutalize mankind; and for my part, I sincerely detest it, as I detest everything that is cruel."[140]

William Miller's youth was no different than that of the other young men of his time. Upstate New York and the Green Mountains were the wild frontiers of the expanding nation. The Miller family settled on the border between two states. They came north with another family, the Phelpses, who practiced their faith in nearby Orwell, Vermont. The Miller homestead was located in Hampton, New York, only six miles from Lake Champlain. Vermont's Poultney River was just a stone's throw away. The family were Baptists and helped establish the local church.[141] Often, the sermons young William attended delivered a Calvinist doctrine, in which commoners were warned to fear an almighty and vindictive God.[142] He scribbled many notes, reflecting on the word of God more than the average person.

Early in life, he apparently dabbled in Deism, the idea that God created the world and then simply let events unfold, like the hands of a clock marking the passage of time. He was married, and Miller was more of a free thinker than others. He wrote, "While I was a deist I believed in God, but I could not, as I thought, believe the Bible was the word of God." He added the Bible seemed to be "a work of designing men, whose object was to enslave the mind of man, operate on their hopes and fears, with a view to aggrandize themselves."[143]

Throughout the southern Champlain Valley, there were many different Christian churches. There were Congregationalists and Presbyterians, who generally required their clergy to be educated. The Methodists and Baptists encouraged participation by some without as much schooling.[144] Interest in those churches skyrocketed in the early 1800s.

William Miller predicted the second coming of Christ would occur in the 1840s. *Public domain.*

After serving in the War of 1812, where Miller was exposed to the hell of war, he returned to Upstate New York. As the years went by, he maintained regular attendance at local church services. The church was the center of a community, and an effective preacher could hold significant sway over a congregation. Miller began studying the scriptures on his own. He took in each Sunday sermon, and during his free time, he engaged in an intense study of the holy book. He spent entire days alone, studying the meaning of it all. On several occasions, his explorations brought him to stay up all night, alone, reading and trying to interpret specific portions of the Bible.[145]

His energy went into answering a very old question: When would the second coming of Christ occur? Uncounted clergy emphasized it in their sermons. Multiple writers also attempted to calculate Christ's return.[146] If Jesus walked the Earth eighteen centuries ago and the Old and New Testaments contained hints about the end of the world, when would it occur? Miller became obsessed with this question.

Calculating the religious apocalypse can take a long time.

It took Miller about two years.

By 1818, he had worked out a basic system. He looked at several biblical references and reinterpreted spans of time.[147] His ministry did not start immediately, and there were still details to be worked out, but he was confident with his predictions. Essentially, he supplanted spans of biblical days with years. This was somewhat consistent within the Bible, as Numbers 14:34 and Ezekiel 4:26 both suggest days mean years. Next, Miller applied Middle Eastern history to his studies. Daniel 2:39–45 relays a vision that four kingdoms will last for 2,300 years. A few biblical scholars, Miller among them, contemplated that period began in 457 BCE, when Babylon no longer controlled Jerusalem; 2,300 years following 457 BCE landed him the range of 1843–47.

He was convinced he was correct but was unsure of how to proceed. Miller did not minister immediately. How does one break the news about the end of world? He discussed his findings with friends and family for years.

There were different levels to his revelations. Believers would join all the spirits, angels and worthy to experience God's love. Nonbelievers, or those who did not live by the Ten Commandments, faced an apocalyptic fate. The good Christians would be with God in heaven. Everyone else would be with Lucifer in hell.

Throughout the 1820s, Miller discussed the future with his family. As the decade passed, he became more certain that he was right. He maintained his association with the Baptist Church.

Approximately thirteen years passed between his initial calculations and when his beliefs emerged in the public realm. Miller thought God had selected him to spread the word of the coming apocalypse.[148]

Tucked in the lower heel of the Champlain Valley, in that unique section of New York on the east side of Lake Champlain, Miller approached local religious leaders. In an eight-page document, he attempted to persuade one of Low Hampton's ministers, Lemon Andrus. He met with partial success and spoke with Truman Hendryx, a Baptist preacher. Hendryx accepted Miller's thoughts about Christ's imminent return and responded, "Go and tell it to the world."[149]

The communities on the lake's southern tip were suddenly under a very religious lens. People were talking about Miller's calculations and looking to the future with a watchful eye. For some, the shores of the lake became entwined with the religious future of Christians, very much like the Red Sea or the Tigris or Euphrates Rivers from ancient texts. The lake shore communities were the first to receive the new word of God. Lake Champlain would become a highway to spread the new word.

Late in the summer of 1831, Miller received an invitation to minister sixteen miles to the northwest, across the lake in Dresden, New York. During the second week of August, he ministered there for about a week.[150] His beliefs were spreading, and audiences were listening. After Dresden, he received invitations to speak all over the region. He was soon in the Poultney, Vermont area, where his message was well received. Then he was in Pawlet, and soon, priests from different congregations invited him to their pulpits. Methodists, Baptists and Congregationalists all sent invitations.[151] He made visits to Granville, Hartford, Salem, Poultney (again), Benson, Brandon, Middletown and Rutland. Like Jesus delivering sermons in the small villages of the Mediterranean, Miller brought his message to the tiny communities along Lake Champlain.

With regional success, he went on the road again in 1832. Some of his letters were published by the *Telegraph*, a Vermont newspaper. He was like a prophet, delivering a message that could save men's souls. His ministry was dubbed Millerism after just five months. He went to numerous towns

A fictional representation of Christ's return, as predicted by William Miller, over a small-town New England church. *Artwork by Josh Sinz.*

in southwestern Vermont and arranged a Canadian speaking tour.[152] His work continued into 1833, and he spent time going between Low Hampton and Dresden, several times traveling the narrows of Lake Champlain. Other area towns and churches encouraged him to speak, including Putnam, Wrentham and Poultney.

Late in the summer of 1834, he traveled north into Upstate New York and was on the road for nearly a month. He preached in the towns of Keene, Jay, Moore's Forks, Keesville and Peru. Miller attempted to maintain a regular life, helping his family during haying season and staying home for the harvest.[153] By October, he'd crossed the lake yet again and was in the churches in Moore's Forks and Keesville. For the first time, he addressed crowds in Plattsburgh, Beekmantown and Wesport. Miller received a death threat in Beekmantown. He was handed a letter signed by ten men who didn't think much of his ministry. The note read that if he did not leave, he would be put where even dogs would not find him.[154] Claiming God as his strength, he returned to Vermont and gave sermons in Pawlet, Orwell and Cornwall.

The Lord gave Miller more strength to spread the word in 1835. He spoke in Addison, Bridport and Shoreham and made plans for an extensive trip through New York. He received so many invitations that it was difficult for him to keep track of them. By March, he was back in Vermont, talking in Bridport and Whiting, and then he was back in New York in the towns of Granville, Middletown and Fort Ann.

Miller's use of prophecies to attract crowds was quite successful. He was often invited by the leaders of other churches to speak. People wanted to see the man who was ministering in the countryside. To round out the year, Miller went into Stillwater in western New York. On his way back, he hit the towns of Bristol, Middletown and Whitehall on the southernmost tip of Lake Champlain. His schedule was always full. In April, he toured central and western New York again.

William Miller had become a prophet very much like John the Baptist prior to Christ's birth. Later in 1835, he spoke in Middlebury and then proceeded northeast through Vermont. He visited several of the communities around Lake Memphremagog in Quebec. Then he went to Troy, Lowell, Eden, Cambridge and Jericho and then went back to Orwell.[155] The traveling took its toll, but by August, he was in communities in New York again. His influence expanded. By the end of the summer, he was on the road again to Lawrence, Stockholm, Parishville, Massena, Fort Covington and Chateauguay. He ended the year back at home.

He was blunt with his descriptions of the future. The crowds came, and Miller delivered. On multiple occasions, he told crowds, "God will arise in his anger." At times, he described death itself: "See, see, the angel with his sharp sickle," evoking images of the Grim Reaper harvesting a crop of sinful, unworthy humans. According to Miller, the end was going to be awful for nonbelievers. At sermons, he said, "Trembling victims fall beneath his pestilential breath," causing assembled churchgoers to think of relatives who didn't go to church. The very air they breathed would be taken from their lungs unless they were saved and bought into Millerism. He did not hold back when he had a crowd. Of the godless nations of the Earth, he said, "See crowns, and kings, and kingdoms, crumbling to dust," and he said society would "see lords, and nobles, captains, and mighty men all arming for a bloody daemon fight." The event would be experienced all around the world: "Behold the heavens grow black with clouds." He would continue,

Christ's predicted return, as it would have looked over the Green Mountains and Lake Champlain. *Artwork by Josh Sinz.*

"The seven thunders utter loud their voices." The end times weren't some far-off date in the future. They were tangible, unavoidable. They would come during their lifetimes.

Once again, Miller set out to spread his revelations. He was on the road again in 1838, with a little more than half a decade left before the end of the world. He received invitations near and far, and he spoke in Troy and Rome, New York. By June, he was back in Canada, and by the end of August, he was on the edges of the Champlain Valley, visiting towns in south-central Vermont. Braintree, White Creek, Pittsfield, Randolph and Brookfield each received visits. Good-sized crowds were common. In November, he spoke in Montpelier. He rounded out the year with visits to Jericho, Stockbridge and then Rochester. He began 1839 ministering in Woodstock, Gaysville and Pomfret. By March, he had visited Essex and Williston. As spring arrived, he was in Waterbury. This was some of the last work he did in the Champlain Valley for some time, as he had been invited to speak in Massachusetts.

Ministering in population centers allowed Miller to attract attention from those who could further spread his word. People began talking, sharing his views, and in Massachusetts, he attracted publishers willing to print and spread his message. He was in Massachusetts until June 1839.

When he returned home in late June, he ministered in Westford, Cambridge and Colchester. In his writings, he documented the many souls he converted to Millerism. He was home for much of the summer and worked on his fall speaking schedule. His attention returned to southern New England.

Miller went back to Massachusetts and lectured in several towns in October and November. He briefly visited Exeter, New Hampshire, but the response was not entirely enthusiastic. It was on this trip that he met Joshua V. Himes, the pastor of the Chardon Street Church in Boston. Himes invited him to Boston, and Miller spoke at Himes's church. Himes had access to publishers and committed to printing copies of Miller's sermons. In January 1840, Miller went back to New Hampshire. After January 20, Miller's lectures were printed widely in area newspapers. His words were captured in the "Signs of the Times," and his predictions were now available to a larger audience.

A brief trip home followed, where Miller spoke to packed churches. Then he was in New York City. His predictions about the end of the world had started on the shores of Lake Champlain, and now, he was in Boston and New York. After a few well-received lectures, he once again traveled to the Eastern Townships of Canada. As the peak of summer approached, he returned home for a few weeks.

Miller took time to rest, enjoy his family and think about where his future visits should unfold. He settled on returning to places that had given him early attention. He was in Fort Ann, New York, and South Bay, and then he traveled to Colchester, Vermont. Columbus Green of Montgomery attended these sermons and recorded that the pews were full, and he wrote that Miller was "the chosen vessel of the lord." Stops in Burlington, Salisbury and Sudbury soon followed.

The message spread. Speaking engagements in Boston dominated his schedule in early 1841. For more than two months, he spoke to large audiences and reached out to locations he had not visited before. By April, he had visited churches in Providence, Rhode Island. He again returned home for the summer and took speaking engagements in New York for August and September. In November, he returned to New Hampshire and Massachusetts. He was back in Dover, New Hampshire, to round out 1841.

By early 1842, he was all over the place. First, he went to New York in January and then New Hampshire in February. In March, he was back in Massachusetts.

It was now the spring of 1842. While he had never assigned a specific date to the end of the world, he now pushed a narrow range, between March 1843 and March 1844. For converts to Millerism, the spring equinox of 1842 was a concrete marker. Even with the calendar's vagueness, the first possible date for the end of the world was only a year away.

While the movement gained popularity, there were detractors. Some ravaged Miller. The *Universalist Watchmen*, a Montpelier paper, was particularly harsh. In its July 9 issue, it questioned Millerism and Mormonism. Perhaps reacting to his growing crowds, the paper denounced his calculations and accused him of promoting apocalyptic scripture verses just to accumulate followers. With the abolitionist movement growing, the paper sarcastically asked: If the world was ending and the slavers were going to perish anyway, why engage in so much antislavery work?[156]

By this time, other people began to push that the end was inevitable. In July, a man with the last name of Fitch showed up on the streets of Burlington. He ministered publicly, trying to convert people on the streets.[157]

Some churches gladly opened their doors to Miller and supported his ministry; others were confrontational. Some Universalist groups condemned Miller publicly and dubbed him a fanatic.[158] They called him a childish and vain old man and stated his calculations were nonsense. The Universalists may have been concerned that some of their own were now listening to Miller. At this point, the following may have converted as many as half a million people.

Some publications took their criticisms further. In September, the Woodstock, Vermont paper *Spirit of the Age* implied Millerite organizers were just in it for the money. At issue were the subscriptions to print sources that promoted Millerism. *Spirit of the Age* pointed out that if April 1843 was indeed the end, why did followers need to buy a year's print subscription?[159] It also published a point-by-point criticism of Miller's math.

Even the naysayers acknowledged that many people were beginning to convert. One paper noted that when Taunton, Massachusetts, hosted a gathering of Millerites, thirty to forty tents were erected. Estimates said that two to five thousand people attended.[160] The *Plattsburgh Republican* reported that a selectman in an eastern town had given up his elected seat. He was simply interested in getting his affairs in order for the burning of the globe. Another individual was harvesting his crops and let others know that he wouldn't plant as much food again, since everything was coming to an end.[161] In November, the *Middlebury People's Press* ran a story that called out the Millerites. It labeled Miller a "stupid pretender" and reported infatuated citizens had stopped working, arguing they no longer needed to labor with just six months left to live.[162] A few Vermont papers ran snippets in late November, and they flippantly printed that the movement's calculations were based on rainbows and moonbeams. They addressed Miller's math and said the effort went against even basic arithmetic.[163] The next month, the *Middlebury People's Press* was at it again, identifying the new disciples as innocent and harmless persons who should have known better.[164] In the words of the paper, the followers were being "fleeced."

As 1843 approached, some could not cope. In the final weeks of 1842, the *Vermont Patriot and State Gazette* reported unfortunate news from Somerset, Massachusetts. Four women were convinced of the imminent end of the world. Their behaviors changed; they became deranged. One woman died. Another was committed to the Worcester Asylum. The other two were in such bad condition that they had to live with friends.[165]

In West Randolph, Vermont, a formerly good citizen, father and husband became unhinged. He did not talk to anyone unless it was about the second coming of Christ. His interactions with his family became unfortunate, with some observers reporting they lived amid hatred and abuse.[166] That the change hit in the weeks before Christmas, the most important holy day for Christians, which was ironic. The *Vermont Patriot and State Gazette* reported nearly every community had people agitating others.

This didn't occur in the Champlain Valley alone. Near the end of December, the *New York Tribune* reported that several groups of Millerites were banding together in Boston. Their objective was to erect their own building where they could await the end of the world.[167]

At the start of 1843, Millerites everywhere began preparing. Several groups around Middlebury got together and prepared to erect a brick building for the end of times. The main structure was to be about fifteen feet tall, and it would have a thirty-five-foot-tall steeple, reaching to the heavens. The Millerites were erecting their own doomsday church.[168] In Concord, New Hampshire, a man decided to correct a wrong he committed thirteen years prior. In 1830, he stole thirteen dollars from another man. With the end so near, he walked thirty miles and repaid what he stole.[169] In early January, there was a fire in Westville, New York. It occurred in the middle of a snowstorm, and the flames were enhanced by the winds. It brightened the clouds and the surrounding area. One

Millerite got so worked up that he got on his horse, rushed through the community and yelled the world was coming to an end.[170] Other areas of New York suffered through an outbreak of a disease called the "black tongue." Millerites were convinced this was a reference to the spread of diseases close to the end. In late January, two Vermonters, one from Barton and one from Brownington, apparently died from a fear of what was coming. In both cases, they were healthy but had dabbled in Millerism.[171] In February, local newspapers reported on nice displays of the northern lights. They sheepishly reminded people that the bright lights in the night sky were not a sign of the apocalypse and that the northern lights merely occasionally provided colorful displays.[172] Others legitimately claimed they saw the planet Venus during the daytime.[173] Experienced sky watchers understood this was not an amazing occurrence at all, that Venus is almost always visible just before sunset.

With all these sermons and speaking engagements, Miller went to great lengths to explain that he had never specified a single day. His calculations pointed to Jesus's return occurring sometime between March 21, 1843, and March 21, 1844.[174] Up to that point, Miller never offered an exact date.

He continued to minister. Days and weeks passed. Months went by. The end of it all might happen at any random moment.

When March 21, 1843, came and went without incident, many Millerites maintained their faith. Their prophet had spoken in generalities. There was immense pressure to provide a specific date, especially with the early part of the range behind them. Bowing to public interest, Miller quietly suggested the end could happen on April 18, 1844.[175]

When that date passed, public scrutiny mounted. Fourteen years into his ministry, Miller was being branded a phony and fake.

Bowing to further public pressure and attempting to explain away his earlier miscalculations, Miller relied on math from other members of the movement. Another Millerite, Samuel Snow, used his original calculations and amended them slightly. He pushed October 22, 1844.[176]

Miller agreed and went public with the date.

The implications were enormous. William Miller had publicly endorsed a date, and that was all his followers needed for their prayers to be answered. They wanted and needed Miller to be correct.

They would be saved.

As the date approached, the Millerites rejoiced. Some people stopped tending their fields and animals. Others talked about places to gather to witness the great event.

During this period, Miller's followers focused on apocalyptic verses in the Bible. They read the language from Revelations 6:12: "And I beheld when he had opened the sixth seal, and, see, there was a great earthquake; and the sun became black as sackcloth of hair, and the moon became as blood." Another Bible verse with similar imagery was Matthew 24:29: "Immediately after the tribulation of those days shall the sun be darkened, and the moon shall not give her light, and the stars shall fall from heaven, and the powers of the heavens shall be shaken."

Another that undoubtably grabbed attention was Joel 2:29–31, which reads, "And also on the servants and on the handmaids in those days will I pour out My spirit. And I will show wonders in the heavens and in the earth, blood, and fire, and pillars of smoke. The sun shall be turned into darkness, and the moon into blood, before the great and terrible day of Jehovah come."

Even darker was Matthew 24:7–8, which says, "For nation will rise against nation, and kingdom against kingdom: and there shall be famines, and pestilences, and earthquakes, in diver places. All of these are the beginning of sorrows." Believers wondered if the crops they had planted in the fields of Colchester, along the riverbeds of Otter Creek or on farmland in Benson, was even worth it. Miller's followers may have been waiting for earthquakes, and they were probably paying special attention to the moon.

All these predictions led to what history remembers as the "Great Disappointment." The second coming did not unfold on October 22, 1844. Followers of Miller waited expectantly in their homes. They looked to the heavens on that night, hoping his prophecies would be fulfilled. In the aftermath, Millerites had to deal with their own shattered expectations and intense public pushback. Many just left their faith, mistaken, shamed and vulnerable.

Miller continued to minister and still believed that the second coming was imminent. He went north and south, up and down Lake Champlain. He died believing what he had predicted would still happen.

Thankfully, William Miller was wrong.

10

THE CAPITAL OF THE NORTH

First constructed in 1890, Hotel Champlain quickly became one of the most attractive resorts in the Champlain Valley. It received notoriety because of its size and hospitality, but it also became the summer vacation spot for President William McKinley.

At the time of her husband's presidency, Ida McKinley was not well. She was emotionally decimated after trying to raise children and take care of her family. The couple had their first child, Katie, in 1871. They enjoyed being parents. Their second child, Ida, was born in 1873. Sadly, she lived only a few short months. Mrs. McKinley was devastated and never recovered from this tragic loss. To make matters worse, in 1875, four-year-old Katie came down with typhoid fever and died just days later. Mrs. McKinley was emotionally broken and succumbed to seizures, phlebitis (inflammation of the veins) and epilepsy. The doctors of the time prescribed medical doses of barbiturates and laudanum, both of which likely contained opium.

Their first visit to the north country occurred in 1897. Hotel Champlain was informed it would be hosting McKinley in July. The president wanted a safe and healthy atmosphere for his wife during their time away from Washington. It was organized as a working vacation, as Vice President Hobart and members of the cabinet planned to spend at least part of the time with the president.[177] The hotel was informed that the stay was to be for a month, beginning around July 28. The vacation could be extended two weeks into September, depending on McKinley's schedule and the First Lady's health.[178] The oval office requested the hotel provide living

One of the most unique hidden stories of Lake Champlain; McKinley visited and saw the North Country as a second home. *Library of Congress, public domain.*

arrangements that allowed some level of isolation for the president. The resort was happy to honor this request. Part of the hotel's allure was its views of Lake Champlain and the Green Mountains of Vermont. Plattsburgh's military barracks were half a mile away.

As the time away approached, more details were released. The hotel arranged the presidential accommodations in the annex, which connected with the main hotel via a large sun parlor. The staff arranged for Mrs. McKinley's accommodations to have blue and silver walls, colors she found calming. The president's interest in Upstate New York may have hinged on the influence of his vice president and his staff. Vice President Hobart was a regular patron of the hotel for years, and he spoke highly of the location.[179]

The first family announced further arrangements on Monday, July 26. They would be in Washington until Wednesday and depart by train for the Champlain Valley at noon. They would arrive in Plattsburgh at 6:00 a.m. on July 29. An assortment of cabinet members, family and staff accompanied them. Mrs. McKinley's aunt and her maid came along to make the first lady comfortable. At this early juncture, the president intended to try to stay a full six weeks.

With little fanfare, they arrived in Plattsburgh and were taken to the hotel by 7:00 a.m. Everyone enjoyed breakfast before settling in.[180] Mrs. McKinley commented that her accommodations were the exact colors she adored.[181] The first family was housed in a suite of seven rooms on the second floor of the hotel's annex. Their first day was reserved for rest. McKinley's only public appearance was to explore the hotel lobby. He found the "weighing machine" and discovered that he weighed 191 pounds.[182] He took his meals in his room but let the staff know he wanted to take occasional advantage of the public dining room.

Some of his first visitors were from Vermont. General Peck, the adjutant general of Vermont, represented the governor and arrived with orchids, roses and carnations for all the women of the party. With him were General Guy Henry, the commandant of Fort Ethan Allen. Before departing, they received a promise that the president would visit Burlington.

He talked with his staff about the plans for the next week. He would review the Twenty-First Infantry Regiment stationed in Plattsburgh and attend their officer's reception. They spoke of a trip on a steamer to Isle La Motte, where the president would be hosted by Vermont senator Redfield

President McKinley became very familiar with the hotel grounds. *Library of Congress, public domain.*

Proctor. Also on his schedule was a visit to the national guard encampment in Chester, Vermont. Hotel patrons didn't have access to the president. The press reported that there was a "colored" porter at his door at all times.

As president, McKinley could not be in total isolation. He had a polite conversation with the hotel manager, Mr. Seavey, about a reception where the public could call on him. It was the peak of the summer season, and the resort was filled with guests. New York newspapers proudly identified the Hotel Champlain as the "Nation's Summer Capital."

On July 30, the president experienced escapades only the leader of the United States might endure. Locals referred to the hotel as the president's new home, but he desired to get out and about. Around lunch, McKinley and a staff member took a walk around the grounds and thoroughly enjoyed the surrounding woods. In the afternoon, he and his wife arranged for a ride in a horse-drawn carriage. They passed the regimental headquarters of the Twenty-First Infantry. The route was unannounced, and the twenty men on duty, led by Lieutenant Springer, recognized McKinley. They interrupted their work, gave a bugle call, presented arms and saluted the commander in chief. Next, McKinley asked to be taken into Plattsburg. Most of the locals did not identify him. However, McKinley was said to have been watching the eyes of people on the streets. If there was a chance anyone recognized him, he removed his hat and nodded.[183] The afternoon finished with the thirty-five-instrument band of the Twenty-First Regiment going to the hotel grounds. Afterward, Mrs. McKinley went to the west balcony of her residence. For a long period, she enjoyed the farmland and pine forests that stretched toward the Adirondacks. Later that afternoon, the first couple went to the opposite balcony, which faced Lake Champlain and the Green Mountains.[184]

The president's schedule was open the next day. He told his staff he wanted to go fishing and enjoy the golf tournament. He commented that he was looking forward to visiting Vermont.

Ida McKinley decided to interact with some of the other guests. She was alone on her balcony, taking in nature, when she noticed several young girls playing on the grounds. She watched the kids for a time and politely asked them to come up to see her.[185] Many fear gaining weight during vacation, and President McKinley was no different. In these first days, he commented to his staff that he thought he had gained five pounds since leaving Washington.[186] This may have been his motivation to visit the golf course.

On Sunday, August 1, the president's party attended the services at the First Methodist Church. McKinley was given the seat of one of the community leaders. Reverend A.H. Eaton conducted mass. The church was crowded with worshipers from other denominations who came to see their president. McKinley put a silver dollar in the contribution plate. When the mass was over, he stayed and shook hands with people on the steps. In a curious incident, a young man firmly took McKinley's hand and told the president that he had a nice voice. Locals rushed the man away.[187] After the service, the party returned to the hotel. The couple went for a leisurely Sunday afternoon carriage ride through the outskirts of Plattsburgh, along the lake shore and into the open country. The president's day ended with a few visitors, who pressed him to accept an invitation to an Army of the Potomac Ceremony in Troy on August 19. The event was put on his schedule.[188]

The main activity of August 2 was McKinley receiving and reviewing the Twenty-First Infantry Regiment with Secretary of War Alger. The troops paraded for about half an hour.[189] In the next couple of days, another review of the troops was conducted. They once again went to the Hotel Champlain, where they were observed from the balcony. One feature that elicited much enjoyment was the presentation of the regimental bicycle corps. The band played again, their tunes carrying through the grounds under the afternoon sun.[190] At the president's request, the public was let in to enjoy the concert.[191] Preparations were underway for the president's coming visit to Vermont.

Vice President Hobart arrived that night by train and was greeted with fireworks. Vermont lieutenant governor Fisk and John Titcomb, the president of Vermont's Fish and Game League, visited and discussed the details for the coming days in the Green Mountain State.[192]

On August 4, in a sign of the times, there was a press account that said the president was being protected by at least two secret service agents. They were rarely noticed.[193] Their presence was understandable, considering the recent history of violence against the chief executive. Abraham Lincoln's assassination was still a scar on the national consciousness. James Garfield was also killed during his presidency, just sixteen years before, in 1881.

The trip to Vermont began. The president, his wife, the vice president and the rest of the staff went down to the ferry wharf after breakfast. They were joined by approximately sixty members of the public, whom the president simply invited on the ferry ride.[194] They gathered on the *Maquam*.[195] The ship took them south and east across the broadest section of Lake Champlain. It arrived in Burlington at noon, and the dignitaries were given a near-royal welcome.[196] Before leaving, they were treated to a large meal with local politicians. The party traveled by carriage to Fort Ethan Allen, where the president honored the Third Cavalry Unit. Cannons were fired, trained horses were on display and the group was greatly impressed. Mrs. McKinley, however, became very fatigued. She became so feeble that she needed help walking with the president.[197] The steamer *Vermont* brought everyone back to the Hotel Champlain, and she immediately retired for the evening.

The presidential schedule included trips to Ausable Chasm on August 5 and the much-anticipated visit to Isle La Motte on August 6. While the Ausable Chasm trip had been talked about with the staff, nothing was set in stone. The first family told everyone they were fatigued and that they just wanted to spend some time alone in their residence. Everyone else left to enjoy Ausable Chasm. William and Ida McKinley emerged from their quarters and asked for a personal carriage. The hotel arranged one, and they just took off. Around 5:00 p.m., locals celebrated the Plattsburgh baseball team's victory over Burlington with a score of 22–0. Locals were enjoying their victory, and awkwardly, the president and his wife arrived in the area. They moved on, as McKinley wasn't much of a baseball fan.

When McKinley returned to Vermont, he brought a smaller group with him. They were once again ferried on the *Maquam*.[198] Vermont dignitaries

Occasionally, the president and Mrs. McKinley were able to enjoy a carriage ride. *Library of Congress, public domain.*

spoke of the state's history, and McKinley was impressed with the beauty of the Lake Champlain Islands. Vermont was one of the first states to support him during the Republican nomination process. Hundreds of Vermonters greeted him in Isle La Motte. Senator Proctor and Vermont governor Grout attended the event.[199] A lunch was held, cooked by Vermont women, and the president explored the grounds of the Fiskes' property. In the afternoon, the steamboat *Reindeer* arrived from Burlington, carrying members of the Fish and Game League. After the extraordinary dinner, the presidential party got on the *Maquam* and returned to Plattsburgh.

August 8 was a day of a few meetings, but McKinley was convinced to go bowling by the vice president.[200] The lanes were located in a building not far from the annex, and the two American leaders enjoyed their competitive time alone. The vice president won the game, handily beating his boss 187–115. That evening, the hotel put on a state dinner for its guests. The president attended the Presbyterian church services in Plattsburgh on Sunday and tried to relax. Sometimes, the commander in chief being on vacation doesn't always work out, as he received news of the assassination of Spanish premiere Mr. Canovas. McKinley was horrified but didn't offer an official comment.[201]

The next week delivered a lot of work. On Monday, McKinley crossed the lake and was in Burlington again. On Tuesday, the schedule was full, with a visit to the Catholic summer school in Plattsburgh and then a legitimate visit to Ausable Chasm. On Wednesday, he went to Lake Placid, and in North Elba, he visited the tomb of the militant abolitionist John Brown. That Thursday and Friday, he went back to Vermont. He dined with Senator Proctor at his home, and on Friday, he was in Rutland visiting the national guard encampment. After attending a ceremony in Chester, Vermont, the President promptly returned to the Hotel Champlain for a little more of his vacation.

Saturday, August 14, saw a return to some low-key time. McKinley received and dined with various cabinet officials and politicians but didn't have much on his schedule. He attended religious services in Plattsburgh that Sunday.

On Monday, August 16, he reviewed the Twenty-First Regiment at the Plattsburgh Barracks. The president received a historically priceless gift from Colonel Martin. It was an oak ruler. For weeks, McKinley got up each morning and looked southeast toward the beautiful Valcour Island. Benedict Arnold's fleet had fought the British in there in October 1776. During the fighting, Arnold's flagship, the *Royal Savage*, ran aground on the southern portion of the island. Parts of its hull rested among the rocks for over one hundred years. Colonel Martin retrieved a piece of its hull and then crafted the ruler. McKinley accepted the gift and stated it would be used in the senate chambers in Washington at the opening of the next session.[202] The McKinleys informed the hotel that if circumstances permitted, they would like to return the next summer. All good things must come to an end, and the McKinleys started to think about the end of their vacation.

On August 19, presidential duties pulled McKinley away from the "Capital of the North" again. In the evening, he was on a train to Troy, New York. It was the reunion of men from the Army of the Potomac during the Civil War. The president was back at the Hotel Champlain by Saturday morning.

It was the final Sunday of their vacation. The president had breakfast and quietly attended the religious services offered at the hotel. On Monday, August 23, he breathed in his final views of Lake Champlain. The time away from Washington had rejuvenated the president. The president and the first lady had immensely enjoyed their time, but all good things must come to an end. The final scheduled items were an official final review of the Twenty-First Infantry Regiment and the preparations for departure. McKinley said, "I never enjoyed an outing in my life more than I have here. It is a beautiful spot to spend a vacation, and everything has been done for our comfort. Both Mrs. McKinley and I have improved in health and if possible, would stay here longer." The first couple had experienced what many locals already knew. Few places match Lake Champlain's beauty.

The family was not able to return in 1898. Presidential duties and commitments prevented it. However, their dreams of returning came true in the summer 1899. They announced their vacation plans on July 20.[203] Their expected arrival would be around August 1. A major reason for their return was Mrs. McKinley's health. The administration stressed that Ida McKinley wanted to recover in absolute peace and quiet.

Some of the final loose ends in Washington involved dealing with two of the U.S. government's territories acquired during the Spanish-American War. Spain's colonial possessions in the Caribbean had been taken over by the United States. Puerto Rico and Cuba were going through transitions, and McKinley's work involved organizing civil governments for both islands. Another demanding topic was another former Spanish colony, the Philippines. McKinley told his staff he wanted to build a civil government there, too, but an ongoing insurrection forced a postponement of those plans.

Additionally, the president had replaced his secretary of war, Russell A. Alger. The resignation was put on the president's desk on July 20, just prior to the McKinleys' trip north. Eliot Root had filled the position and had been conferencing with the administration all week.

The party departed Washington on Thursday, July 26. Hundreds of people were at the train station to witness his departure. Members of the administration saw them off. The trip started with little public attention, as McKinley specifically requested that no press be allowed in the train car with him. His wife and his niece Miss Sarah Duncan were with the president. Suffering from bouts of fatigue, Ida was able to stand during the first leg of their journey. The first couple requested the same accommodations they enjoyed in 1897. The journey lasted through the night, and they arrived at 8:45 a.m. The first lady was described as pale and weak. It was a storybook arrival, however. A carriage pulled by two horses picked them up. It took them up the long driveway to the hotel, where the presidential flag was raised above the grounds. As they walked up the steps, the hotel orchestra played "The Star-Spangled Banner" and "Hail to the Chief." After the greetings were out of the way, the McKinleys retired to their rooms, which had been repainted blue and adorned with flowers, pleasing the first lady. Not long after settling in, McKinley was seen on the first-floor balcony sitting in a rocking chair, smoking a cigar.[204]

The first day was meant to be a quiet one. The president was observed walking around the hotel property alone, enjoying the trails, the park and solitude. Ida was seen observing the lake. Not long after arriving, the president was forced to resume his official duties; President Heureaux of Santo Domingo had been assassinated, and the news arrived by telegram. The staff cabled back a quick response, expressing condolences for the loss of the foreign leader.[205] The president retired early, and the staff remarked to the press that Mrs. McKinley's first night gave her the most restful sleep she'd had in six months.[206]

The next day, July 29, began with McKinley taking a long stroll with his niece and private secretary along the shore. He came across other hotel patrons, who asked if he would like to enjoy a game of golf in the afternoon. The president approached the steamboat wharf and encountered an old man who was fishing. They chatted with the old fellow for some minutes. The elderly man caught a six-pound pickerel and presented it to the leader of his country.

McKinley's staff informed him of numerous invitations from Vermont, but he politely declined them. He would not fill his schedule while his wife was getting much-needed rest. The first weekend elapsed, and the president decided not to attend church services.[207] This may have been because of the unexpected cool temperatures, barely above fifty degrees.

A president on vacation is never really on vacation. July 31 started with McKinley's staff sifting through mounds of accumulating mail. Given the hotel's proximity to the Canadian border, which was just a few miles away, it seemed appropriate to host the Canadian prime minister Sir Wilfrid Laurier. A dispute had arisen between the United States and Canada over the Alaskan border, and a meeting was needed.[208] McKinley was made aware of an outbreak of yellow fever in Hampton, Virginia, and directed that every effort be made to avoid the spread of the disease. The president also needed to entertain, and in the afternoon, he received Colonel Cannon of Vermont. The officer brought two of his horses over on a steamer for McKinley to observe. The president's staff was surprised with his ability to handle the large animals.

Members of the president's cabinet joined him at the Hotel Champlain on August 1. For entertainment, they were expected to observe a golf tournament that afternoon.[209]

On August 2, the president met with members of the Twenty-Sixth Infantry Regiment. While back at the hotel, he complained to his staff that he had developed "Kodak Friends." McKinley didn't like the number of people who had tried to take pictures with him.[210] Still, he hosted local Republican politicians and associates from the military.[211] Vacations are meant for families to relax. On this occasion, it was the president's brother Abner McKinley who visited for a short time. Vice President Hobart and his family were on schedule to join him as well.[212]

McKinley didn't want to miss church again. He wanted to attend the Methodist services in Plattsburgh, but the driver mistakenly brought him to the Presbyterian church. Fifteen minutes later, McKinley was at the right service, and it had been delayed for his arrival. Later, the McKinleys and Hobarts enjoyed the waters of Lake Champlain. They took in the boat races on board Mr. Webb's yacht.[213] The races featured craft from the Lake Champlain Yacht Club.[214]

On August 9, the president promised he would visit the local Catholic Schools of America, where he would conduct a bit of diplomacy. Two English and Canadian military officials received an audience.[215]

Foreign policy issues dominated the rest of the day. The new secretary of war arrived and met with McKinley. Events in the Philippines demanded his attention. Rebel groups fighting against the colonial interests that dominated the region had made trouble for American policymakers. After their meeting, Secretary Root stated, "The war in the Philippines will be prosecuted with all possible energy. All the men, all of the arms, and all of the supplies necessary to end the trouble in the islands will be furnished at the earliest possible moment." The president wanted to deploy fifty thousand American troops—and more if circumstances warranted. Root inspected the Twenty-Sixth Infantry, the same regiment that had greeted McKinley upon his arrival. They would be sent to the Philippines as part of the war effort.[216]

Vacations can be at the mercy of the weather, and August 1899 was cold and wet. On August 10, the McKinleys stayed in the hotel due to the persistence of the rain.[217]

With two weeks away from Washington, there were press accounts about the president's desire to provide his wife with a quiet and low-key vacation. Ida McKinley's activities and state of mind were constantly mentioned. The typical account was that she sought a place that encouraged good health.[218] McKinley received updates about the foreign policy issues. He received a firsthand account from General Carpenter, who had just returned from Cuba.

The stature the president bestowed on the Hotel Champlain became obvious when another resort in Chautauqua, New York, attempted to lure him away. There were numerous communications, one including details of a private railcar to transport the first family.[219] McKinley declined and was satisfied to keep his wife isolated and safe on the shores of Lake Champlain.

August 13 marked a turning point, as McKinley was about to get into a more regimented work schedule. His wife's condition was greatly improved, and she was in high spirits.[220] The *New York Times* ran a full-page photograph story with six images detailing the president's work and commitments in Upstate New York.[221]

August 14 provided some relaxation, as the first couple enjoyed the return of the sun and warm weather on the yacht *Elfrida*. With them was John Marin, who had been a special deputy collector of customs for the Champlain District for thirty years.[222] They spent six hours on the lake and enjoyed lunch on the water.[223]

When the president attended the Catholic Summer Schools event, thousands of locals came to see him.[224] He had not intended to speak but offered a few words to the crowd and kids in attendance.[225] The Champlain hosted members of the Admiral Dewey Testimonial Fund. They wanted McKinley to visit the New York Metropolitan Opera House when his vacation was over.

At times, Ida McKinley desired fresh air, so the president took her for walks by the golf course. When her health issues resurfaced, they sometimes avoided social events.[226] Plattsburg citizens noted how often members of high society appeared. Escorted by their husbands, women wearing handsome gowns showed up from across Upstate New York.[227]

On August 17, the Plattsburgh Barracks Band provided a summer concert for McKinley and his wife. She still was not feeling well, and the president conversed with the musicians, thanking them for raising his wife's spirits.[228]

The solemn duty of honoring the military didn't cease. McKinley visited the Twenty-Sixth Infantry Regiment again. The soldiers marked his arrival by firing off an old cannon. The men were drilling for their upcoming tour in Manilla, which would start in about two weeks. New York congressmen L.W. Emerson visited as well.[229]

The president's schedule was rarely light. His work visited from Washington, D.C., when he hosted Secretary of State Hay and his wife, Postmaster General Smith and his wife and the secretary of the interior.

August 19 was reserved as a quiet day, and McKinley simply rested in his room until the early afternoon. Later, he was scheduled to go sailing.[230] Mrs. McKinley was feeling good enough for an afternoon carriage ride and joined him on the water.[231]

McKinley hosted then-governor Teddy Roosevelt on August 20.[232]

McKinley was visited by Secretary of War Root, and they conferred about the Philippines.[233] They discussed the recent call-up of ten more regiments and their coming deployments.[234]

By August 25, the president had spent four weeks in the Champlain Valley. It was his final day, and it was going to be a busy one. He observed the Twenty-Sixth Infantry Regiment's band in the morning. After lunch, he was serenaded again, this time by Sherman's Military Band from Vermont. At 3:00 p.m., he observed the 1,300 soldiers of the Twenty-Sixth Infantry Regiment, many of whom were about to be deployed to the Philippines.[235] The original review had been scheduled for the night before, but the rain had postponed it.[236] Before leaving, McKinley tipped the hotel staff generously. The workers were quite excited by his generosity.[237] The president's party entered carriages and were brought to the train station on the hotel's property. With his vacation at an end, McKinley stood on the back platform of the private presidential railcar, the *Cleopatra*, and waved goodbye to the crowds of Plattsburgh.[238]

THE VALCOUR ISLAND COMMUNE

Another interesting story in Lake Champlain's history is that of the Valcour Island Commune. In the 1870s, it was an attempt at a new way of living. This came a century before the era commonly identified with communes, the 1960s and 1970s.

People have always pondered if civilization can be improved. Various thinkers, workers, writers, philosophers and politicians have examined capitalism, democracy, marriage and other institutions. Some have theorized about alternative ways of organizing society. Some have used the Bible to argue that everyone should live simpler lives. Sir Thomas Moore wrote *Utopia*, in which he explored a perfect society. In the middle of the nineteenth century, Henry David Thoreau published *Walden*, in which he documented living in nature. He asked people to consider living more deliberate lives. Nathaniel Hawthorne wrote the *Blithedale Romance*, its setting based on Brookfield in the 1840s, where writers and philosophers tried a different way of life. Marx wrote the *Communist Manifesto* at about the same time.

There was an attempt at a totally new way of living right here on Lake Champlain. While information on the community is scarce, it popped up in a location steeped with historical significance and patriotism: Valcour Island.

This is the same island where Arnold's small fleet hid as the British invaded from Quebec in 1776. The Battle of Valcour is one of the most significant events in U.S. history. About one hundred years later, a revolutionary group of thinkers thought the island could be a free love and agricultural commune.

It is not mentioned in any history books. The idea came from people with little association with the Champlain Valley. However, the organizers were educated and would have studied the writings of Thoreau, Marx, Hawthorne and Sir Thomas Moore.

The pioneering group came from a group of thinkers, the Society of Advanced Spiritualists, and initially came from midwestern states. Prior to putting their ideas into action, they wanted to spread the word about their effort. They had plans for their new way of living. Participants would have specific roles and duties. What they could not fill with people they already knew, they hoped would be filled with some Vermonters. For their revolutionary property, they intended to build at least twelve housing units. From the start, they believed the project's labor would involve caring for fruit trees and horticulture.[239]

Despite some early differences of opinion, by July 24, 1874, concrete efforts were underway to establish the colony. Three individuals, Orrin Shipman, Colonel John Wilcox and O.C. Hall, tried to recruit from different Spiritualist communities in several states. Wilcox had authored *The Approaching Conflict*, in which he predicted a revolution, and from the fighting, an "Empire of Love" would emerge.[240] His writings included pleas for "peace and harmony to overcome the current state of chaos." Fliers and advertising were spread among free thinkers in Wisconsin, Illinois and Iowa. Some writings speculated about what they could do with a property like Valcour. Wilcox promoted that there would be summer bathing facilities and skating in the winter. He noted that while the community wanted to remain in isolation, steamships would be visible on Lake Champlain. He stressed the productivity of Valcour's soil, advertising the best temperate fruits would be available there. Interested parties were to respond by mail, to PO Box 13, Winooski, Vermont. Colonel Wilcox hoped forty-five to fifty families would be willing to settle on the island.

Orrin Shipman was a well-known local in Vermont and was, at first, only loosely tied to the project. His agricultural efforts had produced moderate successes. His property was about two miles from the village of Winooski and was populated with cattle and numerous fruit trees. Shipman sold young fruit trees to farmers. His gardens produced many vegetables, especially onions.[241] Initially, there was speculation that one hundred of his acres in Winooski would be available to the project.

The organizing started in the late summer. The *Burlington Weekly Free Press*, in its September 11 edition, explained what was brewing.[242] Its correspondent had caught wind of the endeavor and set out to investigate. Some of the

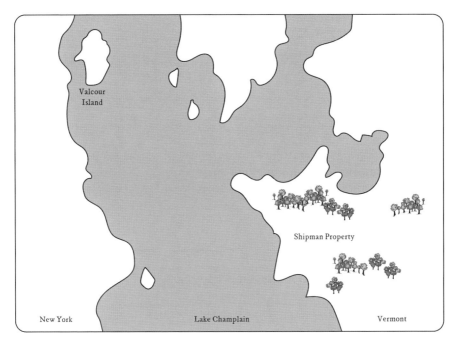

Map of Lake Champlain showing the Shipman property and its association with the Valcour Island commune effort. *Artwork by Lindsay Didio.*

organizers were from Chicago. They were identified as Spiritualists and "free lovers." The leader of the group who wanted to lay down roots was a man named Woodhall.

Another man, Mr. Jones, formerly from Barre, Vermont, published two spiritual magazines in Chicago. Among the organizers, he was not a fan of the Valcour initiative. He saw comparisons with the Oneida Community, which he said was "beneath the highest plane of social morality." That effort had been established in 1848 and featured communal living and group marriages.

Seventeen individuals departed for Vermont from the Midwest. A few left on steamships, and some took rail lines. A few young families made up this group of free-thinking souls. There was G.E. Charles with his wife and child, John Bentley with his wife and child and Mr. Nelson with his wife and at least two children. There was Mr. Lyman and his wife and Ms. H. Augusta White and her two brothers. There was Mr. Woodhouse, who was young, educated and full of enthusiasm at the age of twenty-two. He was the companion of Ms. White and would join the effort by late August. Commenting on the free love venture, Woodhouse said that if Augusta White selected another man before he got to the island, he would not like it, but it was for her to decide.

The local press became very interested in the initiative. The *Rutland Herald* provided a history of social reform and referenced early historical attempts at communal living. They referenced Brook Farm, the mid-nineteenth century effort by several intellectuals and writers to live and work together.[243]

There were reports they would share eight hundred acres on the island, with another two hundred on the mainland. This was Mr. Shipman's land in Colchester and Winooski. After weeks of speculation, details emerged. Agricultural pursuits would be the main labor on both properties. Private property would be limited, and the economics would revolve around one's manual labor. The homes had not yet been built, but the organizers speculated they would be built on the flat plateau on the north side of the island. Each dwelling would accommodate sixteen people. Each housing unit was to have two superintendents, one man and one woman. The community's other roles were those of the secretary and treasurer. Anyone over fifteen could vote, and the government would come from an elected board established by the population of the island. Labor, from the beginning, was to be enjoyed and practiced for the overall benefit of the community.[244]

Reporters, intrigued by the effort and fascinated by its non-monogamous relationships, asked some difficult questions. One pondered if Ms. Augusta White might be a mother in nine months. The reporter wondered if the commune would care who the father was. To this, Mr. Woodhouse responded that when the child was old enough, he could say that all the men were his fathers.

Woodhouse explained that everyone had energy and was accustomed to labor. It was their goal, he said, to make Valcour Island the envy of the world. The use of the property had been arranged by Mr. Shipman. The initial agreement stated that if the venture failed, the property would fall back to him.

Distant newspapers took interest in the project. On September 24, a correspondent for the *New York Herald* was in Burlington and sought out the community's organizers. He took a horse and buggy into Colchester and Winooski. Mr. Shipman's agribusiness, the Champlain Nurseries, was nearby. He met Mr. Wilcox and Shipman, but the meeting did not go as expected. Shipman's twenty-seven-year-old daughter, Isabella, had recently died of rheumatic fever.[245] Friends and family were planning the services. The funeral was to be held in Burlington, and members of the Valcour Community attended.

What followed was a learning experience for all involved. Shipman was sympathetic to the Valcour group and publicly stated that he might join

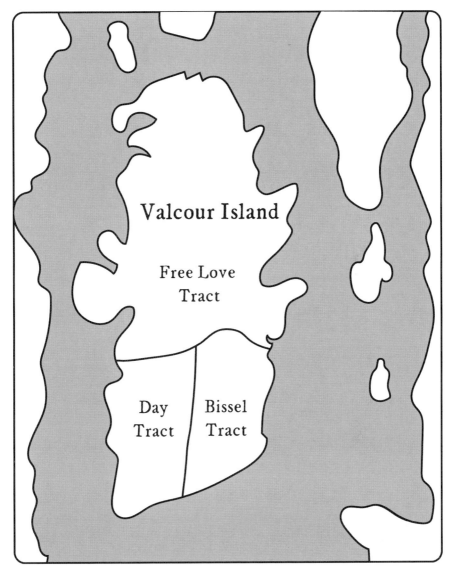

A map of Valcour Island and the areas that the Valcour Dawn Community planned to work on. *Artwork by Lindsay Didio.*

them. The reporter met with Mr. Lyman, who was a professor. Lyman was already not happy with the state of the project. He thought Shipman was asking investors for too much money and revealed that nothing was ready. The building in Winooski, which was to house people as the island work was completed, was not done. Lyman planned to go home and return in the spring.[246] He wanted the venture to attract three hundred participants. The reporter left, hoping to be able to visit the island.

By October 1, with the summer leaves transitioning to fall colors, participants were on Valcour. They had gone fishing to work on their self-sufficiency skills and caught a few pickerel.[247]

The group realized there was not a wave of free thinkers and free lovers arriving after them, so they decided to use the Shipman property as a base of operations. Every Sunday, they held public sessions, trying to attract newcomers.[248]

By October 5, nearly two hundred people were on the Shipman property, most of them just curious. Some may have been sympathetic locals. What followed was one of the more interesting public meetings ever held on Vermont soil. Mr. Shipman, Professor Bentley, J.H. Woodhouse, Augusta White and Colonel Wilcox all represented the commune and spoke from a small platform.[249] They said recent press accounts were inaccurate. Colonel Wilcox spoke of slavery's abolition and how it was progress for the country. Their Valcour effort was just part of that progress. He explained that the group was pushing against the caste system and that industrial wealth was responsible for a lot of pain and suffering. Like Marx or Engels, he argued that real wealth came from physical labor, not gold, greenbacks or bonds. Industry was going to be redesigned so that it was cooperative rather than competitive.

Ms. White addressed the crowd and was awkwardly direct, asking, "Is it possible then, that the people of Vermont, that glorious old champion of freedom and equality, are ignorant of the progress being made in the world of ideas?" She stressed the group believed in the brotherhood of all humanity and that the old social and economic systems were not a good use of time.

Their goals were quite lofty. By October 17, 1874, many had arrived at the Shipmans' property. The organizing for the "Valcour Dawn Community" was well under way.[250] However, some of the new arrivals thought misinformation had been used to get them involved.

Another reporter soon investigated. Two weeks had passed since the meeting at the Shipmans', and more members relocated to the island. The newsman got on a boat and sought them out.[251] The main farmhouse was visible from the water between the island and the New York shore. It was one and a half stories tall. The western dock was decaying, and a rotting cattle boat was already moored. The writer was greeted by an unnamed member, and he asked if Augusta White was available. They walked to the house,

The commune's main farmhouse, located on the west side of Valcour Island. *Artwork by Lindsay Didio.*

where homesteading activities were already underway. The main floor was made up of a single large room. Two women were rolling bread dough. The woodstove threw enough heat to make the room comfortable. The reporter met several people and then was given a tour by Mr. Woodhouse.

The tour revealed the beauty and isolation of the island. The reporter inquired about the free love effort. Woodhouse responded that two people enjoyed each other as much as they desired, and then if they agreed, they simply moved on. As they walked over grassy fields and among trees that featured near peak foliage, it was stressed that interested persons would bring worthwhile skills with them. Woodhouse said he was a carpenter and reiterated they wanted to make industry cooperative, not competitive. Another man stated they had found a version of paradise. He excitedly claimed the island would provide all the lumber needed and that the next growing season, they would harvest potatoes from Valcour's rich soil.

Interest from the press continued, this time from the *New York Daily Herald*. A reporter visited and spoke with two men. They planned to grow and cultivate corn, wheat and tobacco. They wanted to bring in apple and pear trees for an orchard and were planning a large strawberry patch. The fruits could be used for jams and preserves, and it could bring in money to the property. As the men walked the shores, the reporter observed a few

The Valcour Commune was made up of spiritualists, free lovers and thinkers. Such picnics were probably common. *Artwork by Joseph Smith.*

older barns in disrepair. They came to the slight hill, where the lighthouse was located. The newsman questioned them on the topic of free love. Mr. Woodhouse explained that he was with Mrs. White, but they did not need a ring or ceremony to make the relationship complete. He explained that if children resulted from any partnership and it then dissolved, the community would raise those children.

The men explained what they thought an ideal society would be like. They intended to organize the workers into groups based on individual interests. There would be farmers, people taking care of the fruit trees, bakers, butchers and tailors. Each of these working groups would have representation on the overall council and govern the island.[252]

By November, with the short and cold fall days, the Valcour destination was still not ready. John Wilcox went public with his frustrations about the accommodations and the possible misrepresentation of the enterprise. He put out a call to other Spiritualists and sympathetic architects for a series of group buildings. Press accounts labeled the participants communists.[253] By this time, about twenty individuals had been on the land for several weeks.

More were expected to arrive, with peace and harmony reigning on Valcour. On November 10, despite the disagreements and disappointments, Colonel Wilcox stated that some members would attempt stay the winter. They wanted to prepare parts of the island for work in the spring.[254]

Their activities remained somewhat mysterious during the winter. Locals wondered if these new people could survive out there in the bitter cold. Nothing further appeared in the press until the middle of January. Ms. White, described as the effort's lady superintendent, spoke in Plattsburgh on November 20.[255] The lecture was billed as an exploration of "the needs of the times," and she was to speak about communal living. A follow-up lecture was scheduled for January 21 in St. Albans.[256] However, she became ill, and both talks were apparently postponed.

The absence of news suggests that things had not gone according to plan. By February, some went public with their dissatisfaction, wondering if fraud was involved.[257] As the chilling temperatures and the dead of winter held a tight grip over the Northeast, there was little communal love underway on Valcour. Some members believed that Shipman had overrepresented the value of the land and lured them in with false promises. Shipman's lofty efforts were probably sincere. However, his interest in the Valcour property happened at an unfortunate time. It aligned with the economic Panic of 1873, which sent the United States into an economic depression. Banks failed. Railroads went under. What he thought was possible when the economy was strong became impossible. His finances were so strained that even with the free lovers committed, he considered walking away from the mortgage. Some of those who had moved east were in a worse position. They arrived expecting a new utopian home and but found their own accounts depleted. The tensions were severe enough that several members labeled Shipman a fraud.

To defend his reputation, Shipman went public with his own story.[258] He wanted the public to get a true assessment of the effort. He admitted that he needed investor funds from participants but did not expect interest payments. He wanted the community to succeed and not be looked at through the lens of profit and loss. Shipman explained that it was interesting that the group's internal problems had made it to the press, considering the chatty individual enjoyed his hospitality. He questioned the motives of the negative accounts and implied it was someone who may have been running from their own credit problems. He suggested the sources shouldn't have taken internal issues public.

Despite Shipman's response, there were issues, and it was all over the press. His financial dealings came into question, and the public wondered if he had deliberately misled members of the new community.[259] The *Argus and Patriots*, another paper, assailed Shipman for his potential false representations. It did not let the other members off easy, charging that they had failed to do some commonsense research. It charged that Shipman had questionable dealings going back to his antislavery days, that he collected money for the movement but used those funds for his own uses.[260] Another paper suggested the effort was about to break up.[261] The damage was done. During the third week of February, three more Vermont papers ran negative stories.

All was not lost, however. As the cold of February transitioned to the occasional spring warmth, Augusta White worked to educate locals about free love and the Valcour effort. Feeling better, she rescheduled her talk in Plattsburgh. She was sarcastically referred to as the "High Priestess" of the effort.[262] Part of her tour included at least one speaking engagement in Chittenden County.[263]

Despite the warming weather, infighting among the organizers continued, and the particulars again spilled into the public sphere. By the middle of March, two of the group's main personalities were openly feuding.[264] This time, it was Colonel Wilcox, who had recently been arrested by the authorities at the prompting of Shipman. Wilcox attempted to correct the finances in a direction that might benefit the group and ended up in jail. While behind bars, he told his side of the story, exposing serious problems within the Dawn Community. He said that Shipman was not treating some of the members very well. The strife continued, and some participants wanted Shipman arrested.[265] Wilcox suggested that he mistreated his own family and had been cruel to a six-year-old orphan boy.[266] Wilcox's trial unfolded in the first weeks of March. More facts were revealed. He had angered Shipman by trying to pay off some of the property's debts. When the trial was over, Wilcox returned to the island.[267]

April arrived, and some of the Spiritualists went public with their desire to see the project continue.[268] Mrs. Shipman laid much of the blame at the feet of the community, which she said caused her husband considerable debts. Still embracing the visionary future, she wanted the endeavor to move forward. She stated that they could "rebuild the community on the true principles of social life." When the paper the *News and Citizen* published more of her thoughts, it revealed the circumstances of the previous fall. She defended her husband and acknowledged he wanted investors, but they were surprised when Colonel Wilcox and the others showed up expecting to inhabit the island. With the property's housing not physically ready, most of the free lovers had lived with her husband since the fall.[269] They had taken care of and fed them through the winter. Whatever the arrangement had been, tensions were boiling over in the spring. She pulled no punches. She saw them as "consumers" and "non-producers" and further described them as just "visionary theorists, deadheads, and drones." Even with the public spats, early miscommunications and long months of winter isolation, there had been considerable talk about the labor on the Shipmans' property in Colchester and Winooski. The newcomers had speculated that the delayed island work could be applied in Winooski.

Those long months had not gone well. Mrs. Shipman wanted the world to know that Wilcox was "swindler, imposter, and prince of beggars." Three of the Shipman's boats had been wrecked in the fall of the previous year during quick jaunts to and from Valcour. She charged that many of the free lovers had done little work and that dairy products from their farm had been stolen, consumed or wasted. The miscommunication and inexperience were so bad that when thirty barrels of apples were picked for winter preservation, they were improperly stored and froze in the out cellars. Mrs. Shipman went after the nature of the free lovers, saying their meetings broke down into "frantic revels and orgies." The paper gave Shipman some free advice and said that if the venture were successful, it would need to stay "clear of minds of the liberal and radical stamp." Some of the Spiritualists were on the island in late spring, but things were not going well.

By late spring, the relationship between the Shipmans and the free thinkers had totally decayed. Shipman accused Wilcox of being a "free lust desperado." Of Ms. White, he was equally frank; he said she was a "forger and a fallen woman." Shipman appeared ready to wash his hands of them, even with some still on the island. Much of the equipment had been put up for auction in late May.[270] A magistrate, several prominent lawyers and a local sheriff traveled on the ship *Wanderer* to sell off the assets. A reporter went with them. The sale of the items occurred on the Shipmans' property, where the cattle from the island were gaunt and starving. The reporter wrote that the remaining members were a bit of a disappointment. He had expected to find Colonel Wilcox proud, commanding and willing to have conversations about how to better society. Instead, he found an unshaven, tired individual who was moving animal dung with a pitchfork. The farmhouse, which had served as the living quarters, was in a decaying state. Several chairs were broken, the bookshelves were nearly empty and the inside was insulated with old newspapers. Mrs. White, while sitting in the living area with books and her writings strewn about, commented that the buildings were in worse shape than Orrin Shipman had advertised. Ironically, she added that Valcour was one of the most beautiful places she had ever experienced, and she hoped that something could be worked out for the continuation of the project. Shipman started investigating if other groups could use it as a home base for religious or scientific study.[271]

On June 12, Shipman was still corresponding with others about what to do with the island. It was still his hope that some free thinking community could be set up there, but he had moved on from the previous group. He described the recent effort a "failure."[272]

Aside from Shipman, there was little interest in the free love communal effort. In the year since the intellectual's arrival from Chicago, there were few references to locals even thinking about signing up. The one public occasion occurred in the late summer of 1875. A prominent young man from Williston basically abandoned his family and went to join anyone who remained. By August, there was not much of the effort left.[273]

By October, even Shipman had moved on. He sold the island property to a Mr. Fay.[274] The *St. Albans Messenger* was critical of the entire affair, stating that Augusta White and Mr. Wilcox had been on the island for most of the summer and lived a Robinson Crusoe–type of existence. A year after their arrival in the Champlain Valley, the two moved to New York City, and only stragglers were left on the island. They would be gone in the next couple of days. The *Messenger* decried the attempts of the advanced thinkers and saw them as a "collection of poverty stricken impracticals."[275] The entire effort was going into the ashes of history, along with the unworthy ideas of intellectuals like Fourier and Robert Owen. Half a dozen other newspapers ran the same editorial.

The last to leave the island were Mrs. Morse and Mr. Bentley, who departed during the third week of November.[276] Oddly enough, Orrin Shipman died the same day.[277]

NOTABLE PRESIDENTIAL VISITS

L ocals can understand why Upstate New York, Vermont and the waters of Lake Champlain were a desirable destination for the country's most important politicians. In the modern era, visits from presidential candidates are rare. Tilting the scales against such visits are New York's population centers, located well to the south. And the state's twenty-eight electoral votes always go to the liberal-leaning candidate. It is the same with Vermont's three electors. National candidates look at the electoral math and know they don't need to visit.

However, over the decades, the Champlain Valley has received a significant amount attention from those who have eyed or occupied the Oval Office. Some of their visits are well-documented. Others are mere footnotes, occurring while officeholders traveled between locations. It started after the Revolutionary War. Prior to becoming the first President, George Washington visited the remains of Fort Ticonderoga.

Years later, during Washington's time in office, future presidents Thomas Jefferson and James Madison visited the lake's southern shores. This was in May and June 1791. They went as far north as Crown Point and Ticonderoga. They made a stopover at Chimney Point and experienced the lake as it was starting to become an economic superhighway. Madison noted that the exports flowing into the Montreal market were wheat, flour and pot and pine ash.[278] Jefferson was not impressed with Lake Champlain, believing the waters of Lake George were superior. He wrote his daughter and compared the two, and he noted Lake Champlain was "muddy, turbulent, and yields little game."[279] The future president was tired from his journey and frustrated that poor weather had affected their stay. They sailed about twenty-five miles of the lake and were in the region for a day and a half.[280] Jefferson was a noted observer of agriculture. He was so impressed with the northern forests that he contemplated if Vermont maple trees could grow at his plantation in Virginia.

President James Monroe's visit came in 1817. He traveled by land to the Champlain Valley and was delayed near Burlington. To pass the time, the party took advantage of the services the steamship *Phoenix* offered. Monroe's party boarded the vessel on July 25.[281] The president was honored with the firing of a nearby cannon. He remained on the deck for a quick trip to Vergennes, with the excursion being described as "romantic and delightful." Monroe slept on the *Phoenix* that night. The steamer traveled to the northern reaches of the lake, where he observed the construction beginning at Fort Montgomery. While near the border, he shared a Revolutionary War memory: "I left it a wilderness and now I find it blooming with luxuriant promise of wealth and happiness, to a numerous population."[282] The *Phoenix* brought the commander in chief to Plattsburgh, where his party disembarked.

In 1840, President Martin Van Buren sailed on the Lake Champlain Ferry the *Burlington*.[283]

President Grant visited in 1872 and was ferried by the steamer *Vermont II*.[284]

Rutherford B. Hayes and Grover Cleveland both visited in 1877.

Benjamin Harrison came to the north country in 1891. For part of his trip, he was on the lake, and then he visited Montpelier, Vermont.[285] President McKinley's visits and vacations in the North Country were extensive enough they received their own chapter.

The next president to be in the north country was Teddy Roosevelt, and he wasn't president yet. The interest in Lake Champlain was linked to McKinley, who had spent so much time there. Add the hunting and sporting activities of Roosevelt, and he attended the annual banquet for Vermont's Fish and Game League in September 1901. Roosevelt was now McKinley's vice president, and his trip was about to be forever etched in history. He was a guest of Lieutenant Governor Fiske in Isle La Motte.[286]

Many guests arrived earlier, moving north from Burlington on the ferry *Chateaugay*. They had spent a day in Burlington and then traveled up on the steamer with nearly six hundred people. The vice president's party arrived on the yacht *Elfrida*, owned by Dr. Webb. There were many visitors from St. Albans, Swanton and the neighboring towns. Roosevelt's group consisted of an author, former members of the Rough Riders (his Spanish-American War

Left: President James Monroe visited Lake Champlain during the construction of Fort Montgomery. *Public domain.*

Right: President William McKinley vacationed on Lake Champlain for months during his time in office. *Public domain.*

Unit), a local congressman, a Vermont senator and others.[287] As Roosevelt took a little time away from the proceedings, he received a phone call.[288] He is said to have put the phone down when he received the news and exclaimed, "Oh, my God!"

McKinley was targeted by an assassin in Buffalo. Roosevelt was immediately in communication with the president's staff and was kept apprised of his condition. Vermont's Senator Proctor announced the solemn news to the attendees, and a hush went over the one thousand guests. Roosevelt was in the very same physical location that McKinley had visited just a few years before.

No one knew the status of the president. The report said that McKinley was still alive. The vice president was literally just a few heartbeats away from the presidency. In those uncertain minutes, Roosevelt received an update on McKinley's condition: he was alive and resting. Roosevelt shared the news with the shocked crowd. McKinley's life was in danger, and some of the constitutional authority of the presidency was transferred to Roosevelt the moment the trigger was pulled. McKinley was in pain, incapacitated and fighting for his life. Those conditions necessitated the vice president filling in. Roosevelt announced his intention to leave as soon as possible. He wanted to be at McKinley's side to help him recover. The *Elfrida* brought the vice president back to Burlington, where arrangements were made to transport Roosevelt by rail to Buffalo. While on the yacht, with the weight of the country on his shoulders, Roosevelt said, "On any ordinary occasion I should admire this beautiful sunset and splendid scenery, but I am in no condition to enjoy it now."

Roosevelt left the Champlain Valley, and McKinley held on for several days. Doctors thought his condition might improve, but then he lapsed into

Teddy Roosevelt learned of the assassination attempt on McKinley while he was on Isle La Motte. *Public domain.*

unconsciousness. McKinley died on September 14, and Roosevelt became president. The phone call on Isle La Motte changed Roosevelt's life.

Roosevelt's time in the Northeast didn't end there. He returned to Vermont in June 1902. The initial plans were laid in the early summer; travel through New England in August and September.[289] He went through Vermont via train, with thousands coming out to see the man who had, in a sense, ascended to the Oval Office while visiting their state. The train made stops in various towns, and a large celebration was held in the capital city of Montpelier.[290] By evening, Roosevelt was in Burlington and enjoying the waters of Lake Champlain.[291] He relaxed in Burlington and then went to Thompson's point in Charlotte, right on the lake. He spent about thirty-six hours in the vicinity. He was hosted by Secretary Shaw, and they used the same yacht they had the previous year, the *Elfrida*. Roosevelt spent the night at Shelburne farms with Doctor Webb.

Ironically, Roosevelt had his own brush with death after leaving. On September 3, near Pittsfield, Massachusetts, the president's transportation was struck by a train car. The driver suffered a fractured skull, and one of Roosevelt's secret service agents was killed. The president was thrown to the ground and suffered scrapes, bruises and scratches.[292] He returned in 1912 as part of his progressive "Bull Moose" efforts.

The next presidential visit to Lake Champlain was that of William Howard Taft, who came to celebrate the three hundredth anniversary of "discovering the lake" in 1909. The organizers called on the vast number of craft on the lake to participate in the event and impress the president and the other dignitaries. About two hundred Indigenous people from Canada used a replica village built on top of lake barges as part of a display.[293] Taft's visit was spent on the steamer *Ticonderoga*.[294] He came again in 1912.

Woodrow Wilson visited in 1913 and then again in 1914. Future president Herbert Hoover inspected damage from the flood of 1927. In 1932, Franklin D. Roosevelt had his first visit to Lake Champlain, but he didn't actually enjoy its vast, attractive waters. He was on his way to Vermont for the Rutland County Fair in early September. He took the train up to Whitehall and then traveled by car over the Lake Champlain Bridge into Vermont.[295] He toured several Depression-era work projects in 1936.

The north country has been visited multiple times by other modern candidates and officeholders, but none of them are notable. Current political campaign stops are brief. Candidates are usually flown in and out of a city within hours. Larger states demand so much more attention. That, however, does not change Lake Champlain's history.

Little old Lake Champlain was a haven for numerous past presidents of the United States.

13

THE SPIRITUALIST COMMUNITY AT QUEEN CITY PARK

T he nineteenth century was a time of social and cultural tumult. The rapid growth of cities and the effects of industrialization created new dilemmas for American society. Science gained stature, offering a secular paradigm for understanding the world and the individual, while Romanticism championed truth and beauty as found in art, nature, spirituality and emotion. Social movements like abolition, women's suffrage, temperance, workers' rights, poverty relief and free public education challenged conventional thinking about freedom, justice and equality. While such movements—such as temperance—could be quite conservative and moralistic, radical and utopian ideas also flourished, particularly among the intellectual circles of the North. Freethinkers of the time experimented with communal living, socialism, free love and gender equality.

Several new religious faith groups sprang up, including Mormons, Jehovah's Witnesses, Christian Scientists, Seventh-day Adventists, Theosophists and Spiritualists. Spiritualists believe that the living can communicate with the spirits of the dead and that souls continue to evolve in the afterlife, offering wisdom to the living that benefits individuals and society at large. Although they claim that anyone can communicate with spirits, some people are thought to be especially gifted and often discover their abilities at a young age. Spiritualism's major figures were often psychic mediums who gained fame and sometimes fortune sharing various psychic and supernatural abilities. Some traveled the world, speaking and demonstrating their abilities, while others stayed home, drawing crowds from near and far, eager to hear messages from the dead. Spiritualism provided more public leadership roles to women than many religions did at that time, and it was often intertwined with abolition, suffrage and other reform movements. Among those with an interest in spiritualism were Arthur Conan Doyle, Thomas Edison and Mary Todd Lincoln.

Spiritualism had thousands of followers in Vermont and New York—some merely curious and others devoted believers—as well as a number of nationally famous mediums. Without specific dogma and liturgy, early spiritualism didn't have churches; in fact, some followers continued to attend mainstream churches, blending their Spiritualist views with traditional religious belief. Spiritualists gathered periodically for lectures, séances and at camp meetings in the summer. The neighborhood of Queen City Park in South Burlington was founded as a Spiritualist community and flourished for nearly sixty years.

Located on Shelburne Bay, Queen City Park was owned by the Central Vermont Railroad until 1881. The railroad had built a hotel and dock, and as the area gradually became a popular leisure spot, a number of summer cottages were added. In 1881, members of the Vermont State Spiritualist Association purchased the fifty-acre park and hotel and began holding its annual summer camp meetings there. The Queen City Park Association was established as a stock corporation, with capital stock of $5,000 sold in $100 shares. The association's constitution described its goal "to establish a free platform for the discussion and elucidation of truth, the support of the gospel, and the maintenance of free worship. Also, to establish and encourage true religion and education by developing the social, intellectual, moral, and spiritual nature of man."[296]

The land was adjacent to the Edward Hatch Estate, known today as Red Rocks Park. Edward Hatch summered in Burlington but never lived on the

The beaches of Queen City Park were quite popular during the summer months. *Courtesy of Silver Special Collections Library, University of Vermont.*

The Queen City location was visited by scores of people. *Courtesy of Silver Special Collections Library, University of Vermont.*

estate; it was used as pasture and woodlot until the 1890s, when he created carriage trails that were open to the public.[297] By then, Queen City Park was a bustling summer resort community.

At Queen City Park, the month of August was set aside for the Spiritualists' annual camp meeting, at which time, the population of visitors increased by the hundreds.[298] A Spiritualist temple was constructed for meetings and events. In addition to lectures, "tests" of psychic ability, séances and demonstrations of hypnosis, the camp meeting drew people with wares and services to sell, such as patent medicines and other miracle cures, bottled water from mineral springs, fortune telling, metaphysical books and journals and souvenirs. Spirit mediums used various mystical techniques. Some were called trance mediums, while others used table rapping, Ouija boards, automatic writing or drawing, spirit photography or "materialism," in which a medium was said to manifest spirits in physical form.[299] Séances were particularly popular, perhaps because they provided a greater sense of participation compared to sitting in an audience. Séances involved a medium who would attempt to communicate with the spirits of the dead, either relatives of attendees or other spirit guides who had messages for the living.

Originally designed with 214 tent sites in the park's early days, aggregated lots eventually housed some eighty cottages, many with wide sitting porches and picturesque gingerbread architectural detail.[300] In 1890, the original hotel burned and was replaced by a larger one that was three stories high, with eighty rooms and a dining room for 150.[301] A railroad station in walking distance, livery stables and a boat house and dock provided transportation options to visitors in the era before cars.[302] By the 1920s, a trolley line was established with service every twenty minutes between Burlington and Queen City Park.

There were multiple buildings around the Queen City Park. *Courtesy of Silver Special Collections Library, University of Vermont.*

With a beach for swimming, grassy lawns, a covered pavilion for picnicking and activities and wooded trails overlooking the bay, Queen City Park offered recreation as well as spiritual development. Tennis, cycling, boating, fishing, hiking, croquet and bowling were on offer, as were entertainments such as concerts, dances and recitals. Boat tours of Lake Champlain and excursions by steamer to sites in New York and Vermont were available.

Over time, Spiritualism became less of a focus at Queen City Park, with many original stockholders selling their shares and property or bequeathing it to family who didn't necessarily share their beliefs. The summer cottages were gradually turned into year-round homes.[303] Spiritualism itself was waning in popularity. Professional mediums gave rise to professional skeptics, including Harry Houdini, whose efforts to expose psychics and mediums as frauds received much media coverage. For younger generations, Spiritualism began to seem like a maudlin Victorian fad, while new forms of media, such as radio and film, provided some of the education, entertainment and social exchange that camp meetings had once provided.

On the morning of May 17, 1939, a milkman making deliveries at Queen City Park discovered a building on fire. Residents began forming a bucket brigade and attempted to save their valuables while waiting for the fire trucks to arrive. More than two hundred firefighters came to the scene, and water was pumped from the lake to quench the blaze, but the hotel, a guest lodge, store and several cottages and outbuildings were destroyed.[304] Although the Spiritualists continued to hold meetings at Queen City Park for some years, they did not rebuild the hotel, and the park never recovered as a summer resort. In 1946, shareholders voted to dissolve the Queen City Park Association.[305] The properties were eventually sold to private owners, creating a unique neighborhood enclave near Lake Champlain.

14

PROHIBITION ON THE LAKE

E ntire books have been written about the legal history of alcohol. Over the decades, individual states, cities and counties have regulated the sale of the controversial product.

That changed in the early twentieth century. After years of lobbying, Progressive-era politicians successfully established a national ban. At the end of World War I, Americans amended the Constitution and outlawed alcohol. What followed was one of the most interesting periods in U.S. history. What unfolded was supposed to be completely hidden.

At first, the federal government centered its efforts on interrupting the transport of alcohol over land borders.

For those who disagreed with the law, the Canadian border was very tempting. Canada still allowed the sale and consumption of alcohol. Many Vermont and New York locals were not afraid to dip their toes into this forced black market. They were perfectly willing to cross the border, obtain booze and bring it back for those willing to pay handsomely.

In 1919, just after the ban became law, Swanton, Vermont, was selected as the headquarters for the law enforcement efforts on land. By August, arrests were being made.[306] The amount of alcohol seized—in one case, nearly a dozen twenty-gallon kegs of whiskey—was concerning.[307]

What started on land set the stage for smuggling on Lake Champlain. If the backroads were being used by organized crime, the lake was an opportunity as well. Tensions were elevated in 1922, when government agents came under fire.[308] Agent Walker tried to stop a suspicious car near Woods Hill in Swanton. Shots were fired, and the man escaped into the nearby trees. The vehicle was seized, and a secret compartment was discovered. The contraband was worth several hundred dollars.

Some press outlets, who supported the federal effort to prohibit alcohol, aired their concerns. The *Caledonian Record*, distributed in the extreme northeast section of Vermont, gave attention to the problem on June 24, 1922. In a short but detailed expression of the facts, it chronicled how easy it was to get booze over the border. It said of the clandestine use of boats, "One does not have to worry about customs officials." When getting booze over land became costly, as law enforcement had stepped up its enforcement on the roads, Lake Champlain became very enticing.

On the Vermont side of the lake, it is unclear how much liquor flowed over the relatively isolated waters of Missisquoi Bay. Its only outlet is through a small, mile-wide channel just north of Maquam Bay. The railroad bridge pylons were a barrier for any large craft. However, profit breeds ingenuity. There were several small hotels and resorts in the area that would have profited from patrons looking for a relaxing drink. The Bayview Hotel, the Lakeview Hotel and others wouldn't have minded entrepreneurs getting in their canoes or small boats, going to the bars and establishments in Quebec and returning with black market goods. Their customers would have paid very well for an afternoon cocktail or a drink with dinner.

In 1924, the federal government set up lake enforcement in St. Albans, Vermont. These officers were assigned an impossible task. They needed to communicate with agents in the border communities. Prohibition was six years old at the time, and the tentacles of the black market economy had already reached the best routes. When the agents set up shop, a twenty-six-foot-long motorized craft that could achieve speeds of forty-five miles per hour was brought into St. Albans Bay.

While smaller arrests were made, the first big success of the lake patrols came the next year, in June 1925.[309] As an example of how large the problem was, 1,200 bottles of beer were seized in a scow south of Plattsburgh.

Stepped-up enforcement yielded further results. Not long afterward, men were spotted in a canoe off Isle La Motte. They admitted to border agents that their seventy quarts of contraband had been purchased in Canada. They said they were being well paid and that their destination had been Plattsburgh.

The boat agents complemented searches on land. In August 1925, they reported two vehicles driving suspiciously near the Grand Isle Bridge and radioed in their observations. When police vehicles responded, they seized the first vehicle, which contained twenty cases of alcohol. The police pursued the second vehicle and intercepted it in Alburgh. Thirty cases were found in that one.

By 1926, customs officials had at least two watercrafts at their disposal. One was the *Flopsy Jane*. It was normal for custom for agents to smash the bottles they confiscated.

In 1927, there were major problems with the sheer volume of liquor getting through. By early May, a month after the ice had melted, boats were already being seized. Three were taken in during the first week of May, and one was over forty feet long. John D. Nicholson, the head of customs enforcement at Rouses Point, publicly admitted that lake enforcement was their biggest problem. Officer Kendrick, head of the division, apprehended a boat during the second week of May. He detained a Mr. Anderson from Plattsburgh, whose purpose for being out was obvious. Officers fined him for running his boat without the lights on, not having life preservers on board and not having his pilot's license. In other words, he'd been on the lake to make quick money with alcohol runs over the border.[310]

The year 1927 continued to be busy for the customs agents. On August 19, the 75-foot-long barge *Martin M. Lafontain* moved through customs south of the Richelieu River. Agents observed an enormous amount of farm and animal feed on board and poked around. They impounded the vessel and brought it to the Burlington docks. The press accounts didn't give much detail, but officials suspected "much Canadian Ale" was on board. The barge was towed by the 110-foot-long tug *Robert H. Cook*. The volume of booze concealed in the farm feed was best not released to the press, considering there were six other barges being towed by the tug.[311]

There were countless more violations, both large and small, uncovered by the customs agents. In 1928, the agents stopped a man in a rowboat paddling south off the coast of Alburgh. He had 240 pints of booze destined for Willsboro, New York.[312] In September, customs officials investigated five cars that were parked on the steamship *Vermont*. Agents found about $50,000 worth of illegal alcohol, which outpriced the value of the vehicles.[313] The first large bust of 1929 came in June. A yacht near Isle La Motte's Fiske's Landing was taken in with 480 bottles of ale concealed on board.[314] The men believed they were in the clear, thinking the customs officials worked farther north, closer to the border. When the police got the men to talk, they said the boat had been loaded in New York's Great Chazy River. Such information was critical, because it meant the land patrols were not catching everything. Clearly, stops were being made and booze was being confiscated, but a lot was getting through. The overall 1929 numbers were noteworthy. Customs officials searched about forty boats a month, most of them within a few miles of the Richelieu River.[315]

In 1931, there was a tragic accident that involved the lake patrols. A rumrunning yacht operated by three Burlington men was stopped near Cumberland Head. Before the agents could close, they started to throw their haul overboard. The agents jumped onto their boat, but agent Babcock fell in the lake and drowned. After the fracas, his body went missing for a long period.[316] Flyovers of the lake were conducted in aircraft from the Franklin County Airport.[317]

In October 1931, a customs agent was in the woods near the Canadian border when he observed a rowboat that was floating very low in the water. He watched it for a bit and then called into the customs office. When other agents responded, they found 960 points of ale in the boat. The men from the boat were taken to Burlington and were cooperative with the authorities. One of them, Clifton Flora of Willsboro, claimed ownership of the boat.[318] Willsboro was an intense hub of illegal activity.[319] In one case, three other men, Howard Moors, Charles White and W.C. Hutchins, operated a boat dubbed the *Midnight Sun*. It was also known to customs officials as the *Black Marie*. Officials risked their lives again, as the driver of the *Midnight Sun* fled and never slowed down. The customs boat tried to stop the *Midnight Sun*, and the thugs attempted to escape. When the agents closed the distance, the criminals were observed throwing alcohol into the lake. The officials leapt from their boat and onto the deck of the smuggler while the two craft sped along side by side. There were 672 bottles of Canadian ale on board. The *Midnight Sun* was detained and brought to Burlington, where it was impounded. It was moored at the docks, and officials intended to use it as evidence if their case ever went to trial. Someone familiar with police activities apparently went to the Burlington docks, stole the vessel and sailed it north. A week later, the *Midnight Sun* was found on the coast of Rouses Point, abandoned, its crew apparently having ditched it while avoiding more custom officials.

In June 1932, there was another large arrest.[320] In this case, the lawmen operated near Rouses Point. Three locals operated two boats moving south. James Eddy of Plattsburgh piloted one, and Charles White of Crown Point and Edward Provost of Plattsburgh operated the other. The first boat was fifty feet long and contained 150 cases of Canadian beer. The other was forty feet long and had 75 cases of beer and 50 cases of wine. As officials learned from prior experience, the boats emerged from the Chazy River.

Sometimes, people don't learn from their mistakes, and apparently, Mr. Charles White thought rumrunning was well worth the risk. He was in a downward spiral. His arrest in June didn't set him straight. Two months later, he was at it again, this time with nearly deadly consequences. Customs officials brought their vessel alongside a suspected rumrunner near Windmill Point in Alburgh. It had been a standard patrol, but agents from Alburgh, St. Albans and Rouses Point worked together when they spotted the suspicious boat near the drawbridge. Charles White was waiting with a baseball bat. An altercation ensued, and Agent Izard ended up unconscious in the water after taking several hard blows to the head and body. Only his life preserver kept him afloat.[321] With an officer down, the rumrunner fled south, quickly reaching forty miles per hour. The offending boat was identified as the *Soony*.[322] Officials put out an alert and started searching near Lake George, fearing the craft may have been lifted from Lake Champlain to avoid the attention.[323] Two days later, On August 17, it was found in Otter Creek under some willow trees in the community dock.[324] It was positively identified partially because of a dent in its hull, having been rammed by the government's boat.

Meanwhile, perhaps due to the recent violence, the officials redoubled their efforts on the lake.[325] During the second week of August, the barge *C.H. McKee* and five canal boats were stopped at Rouses Point. They didn't have the facilities to unload all six of the craft, so agents Caswell and Craig lived on the boat for the next week as they brought it over Lake Champlain, down the Hudson River to New York City. About one thousand cases of alcohol were seized.

After the voters changed the Constitution and banned alcohol, the government tried to enforce an impossible law. During that period, Lake Champlain was a hotbed of illegal activity. Good intentions were not enough to deal with human nature. Some people wanted their booze, and they were going to get it. The folly of banning alcohol became obvious after more than a decade of illegal activity. The Twenty-First Amendment repealed the ban on alcohol in December 1933.

15

A Cannon in Missisquoi Bay?

Missisquoi Bay is located in the extreme northwestern corner of Vermont. It is an isolated and remote body of water. Not many younger people have heard about the cannon at the bottom of the bay. It was probably common knowledge at one point, but like an unused book that remains on a shelf, the knowledge was left behind generation after generation.

Interest in the story of the cannon heated up in 2012, when a member of the Highgate Historical Society approached members of the Swanton Historical Society. There had been a public presentation about the War of 1812 and how that conflict affected the area. Gerald Dexter from Highgate offered a question that was steeped in local history: "Have you heard the old story of a cannon at the bottom of Missisquoi Bay?"

At the time, like so many projects that historical societies deal with, the issue remained shelved. The organizations are run by volunteers, and projects need interest to get attention.

Two or three years later, there was another presentation. Mr. Dexter was there again. He loves his history and knows how to keep a research question alive. "Anyone researched the cannon?" he asked, as though the first conversation had never ended.

This time, there was more interest.

What followed became a nice link between town historical societies and Missisquoi Valley Union High School. Mr. Dexter said there were a couple of different stories floating around. According to local lore, old timers had seen it. As best as anyone could recall, there were two or three people who had mentioned the cannon over the years, one of them being former Vermont state representative Steve Beyor, who had recently died of cancer. The other was an older gentleman who didn't live in the area anymore. The gentleman was ninety years old.

Locals in that section of Vermont have the mistaken impression that their home has always been isolated, that it is provincial and nothing ever happened here. That perception is not reality. Northwestern Vermont has one of the most interesting and continuous military histories in North America.

The reemergence of the cannon story represented a chance to connect the past to the present. The Swanton Historical Society partnered with Missisquoi Valley High School to prompt local students to get involved.

After some research, contact was made with the elderly gentleman's family. The story was connected to Mr. John Tracy, who now lived in Vergennes. A date for an interview was established. And the research commenced.

Before the interview, primary and secondary sources were sifted through. With the military history of Missisquoi Bay, it became obvious there could indeed be a lost cannon. Other historical societies and museums were visited. The St. Albans Museum has two cannons in its collection. One was from the Battle of Plattsburgh in 1814. It is not surprising that such a relic made its way back to Vermont. When the British retreated at the end of the War of 1812, they left a lot of their artillery behind. The second cannon, a much smaller one, was found in a barn in Highgate. More research needs to be done on this piece, but it was likely left over from the 1837 Patriot Rebellion in Canada, which spilled over the American border. The overall point: If there were two artillery pieces already left over in the area, could there be more?

The first references to military activity were shrouded in the distant past, anchored in the early French and Indian Wars. The earliest comes from the late 1600s. There is a possibility, albeit small, that a French vessel went into the bay and somehow lost a cannon. Fort St. Anne, built in 1666, was located just a few miles below the southern regions of Missisquoi Bay.

Greylock's Castle, a fort built by the Abenaki in the 1720s, was somewhere in the southern regions of the bay. The French were rumored to have had a temporary military presence along the Missisquoi River, in present-day Swanton and Highgate, but there are no sources indicating how well-armed that group of soldiers may have been.

The French and Indian Wars, however, were a gold mine of possibilities. Swanton was first settled by the French in the 1740s. A sawmill was constructed on the river, and sources suggest a small blockhouse may have been built there. This era had the French constructing Fort St. Frederic farther south. Then in the late 1750s, there was ample opportunity for the French or English to have lost one of their larger guns. The French had constructed a decent-sized fleet at the northern tip of Lake Champlain, just a few miles away at Isle Aux Noix. For months, their vessels patroled the southern areas of the Richelieu River, the lake's northern edge and Missisquoi Bay. The British raided the area, and it is certainly possible that one side lost a cannon. Roger's rangers traveled into the bay. A separate raid on "Wigwam Martinique" even brought one large British warship into the area. Cannon balls have been found on the riverbanks in Swanton.[326] And there were multiple reports of a cannon in the water between the towns of Alburgh and North Hero.

The Revolutionary War also provided numerous possibilities for a cannon to have been lost. In the early months of the war, Benedict Arnold and the vessels *Liberty* and *Enterprise* were just outside of Missisquoi Bay. A few months later, the entire American invasion fleet was just a few miles away. The Americans retreated from Quebec in 1776, and for the rest of the Revolutionary War, there were scouting missions and ships in the area.

The War of 1812 provides the most likely scenario. There were at least four incursions in Missisquoi Bay by the Americans against Canadian and British forces between 1812 and 1814. The first involved American troops gathering in Swanton for the Quebec invasion of November 1812. A better scenario played out in October 1813 and again a month later. American colonel Isaac Clark led warships and raids into the region. In both instances, his ships operated near Duck Point and High Rocks on the Canadian border. The final occurrence comes from another incursion of Quebec in March 1814. Swanton was once again used as a base, and three regiments were deployed in Swanton and Highgate. Artillery was assigned to this small invasion. In the freezing cold, Clark, with several hundred American soldiers and their cannons, marched into Quebec. They used the ice on Lake Champlain as a transportation route, rather than the poorly kept roads. This invasion force was ordered west to link up with a larger force pushing toward the British defensive positions at LaColle Mills, north of Alburgh. A very plausible theory is that one of their guns encountered thin ice, broke through and sank.

The John Tracy interview came next. His account needed to be recorded. The session occurred at his daughter's home in Vergennes. He had not been raised in Missisquoi Bay but spent much of his youth there with his father and uncles. His links to the area were confirmed when he shared great fishing locations and were further cemented when he pulled out old artifacts he found in the region.

John Tracy could have been a teacher. He retrieved an old atlas with water depth measurements. His old hands went through the pages and settled on one that showed the land, shores and waters of Missisquoi Bay. He hunched over and searched for a specific location. His aged and wrinkled finger moved over Swanton. It touched Rock River, and he dragged it to the west. It floated north, just south of the Canadian border.

His account is now an oral history recording kept in the archives of the Swanton Historical Society.

His story begins when he was a young boy fishing with his father. He recalled that it was a sunny day, and the lake bottom was visible. His father told him to look over the side of the boat. John Tracy described seeing a large cannon barrel under six to eight feet of water, partially obscured by mud. This was priceless information. The account matched up with the military incursions researched prior to the interview.

John Tracy was born around 1930. He said the fishing trip happened when he was young. His memory correlates with some of the lowest recorded levels of Lake Champlain. Extremely low water levels were recorded in 1941.[327]

Another aspect of the research was finding out what investigative work had already been done. The Lake Champlain Underwater Cultural Resources Survey was conducted by the Lake Champlain Maritime Museum in the late 1990s. The effort canvased most of the lake bottom to find old shipwrecks, artifacts and other mysteries in the deep. Many were surveyed, but the study ended at the shallow waters of Maquam Bay. Missisquoi Bay had never been searched. If it had been, something like the cannon certainly would have been found. Research opportunities continued.

The Brosky family, who had helped the local historical societies with various projects, lived off Duck Point. The family owned kayaks and a pontoon boat and agreed to help with some reconnaissance. A simple visual survey of the area was conducted, but the only thing confirmed was that there is a lot of water in Missisquoi Bay. The family offered their pontoon boat for future excursions.

The Tracy family was consulted about taking John's story public. They agreed, and his recollections were put on social media. There were plenty of likes and two interesting comments posted by locals.

Further work was done. The Swanton Historical Society explored relationships with a few local divers. The momentum peaked when Frank

Bell, a longtime diver in Lake Champlain, agreed to help the area. Frank's grandchildren attended Missisquoi Valley Union High School, and because of his service in Vietnam, he had been a guest speaker at their high school multiple times. Frank didn't want to be paid; he just wanted to participate in the experience. After looking at the developing research effort, Frank offered to speak with other divers.

The divers, the Broskys and a member of the Swanton Historical Society agreed on a date: October 12. Coincidentally, this was the anniversary of one of the American incursions into Missisquoi Bay during the War of 1812. The search was hampered by the water quality and the reality that Mr. Tracy's memories, while helpful, didn't give a very specific location. It was a needle-in-a-haystack situation. The divers reported the blue-green algae on the water's surface was problematic. The bottom of Missisquoi Bay was nearly impossible to visually evaluate. One of the environmental problems plaguing the region has been sediment and runoff from surrounding rivers. Over the decades, the problem intensified with industrialization, with one study suggesting the depth of the bay had filled in almost two feet since the early twentieth century. The divers searched an area that was approximately eight feet deep. When they returned to the surface, they reported that the lake bottom was very thick and murky. They reported that they could barely see in front of their faces. The search was not successful.

The cannon was not found, but a lot was learned. Better equipment was necessary.

The dives looking for the cannon in Missisquoi Bay have been unsuccessful…so far. *Photograph by Jason Barney.*

Not long after the dive was conducted, Armand Messier of Northern Vermont Aerial Photography was approached to take drone footage of the search area. The drone took close shots of Duck Point, High Rocks and the surrounding water. The drone film did not reveal anything concrete but provided classes and interested parties with a visual reference point.

The next summer, the search for the cannon resumed. Frank Bell's network of divers contacted the historical society and wanted to continue looking. Three more searches were conducted near the location of the first dive, with no positive results.

There is a possibility that the local lore is incorrect.

The work so far has been done for the love of history. With proper planning, a grid coordinate map will be used, and the various dive locations will be recorded.

Divers have commented they would like to volunteer and continue the work.

At this time, research is underway to narrow down the historical references about the military forces deployed in the area. In a sense, the research has already given positive results. When the first inquiries about Missisquoi Bay began, the references to a cannon off the coast of Alburgh had not yet been discovered.[328] Research provides rabbit holes that are hard to avoid.

One thing is certain: the effort, the evidence and the rediscovered references to other cannons have been a reminder of just how vast Lake Champlain's military history is.

16

Nature Trails of the Champlain Valley

The Champlain Valley is fortunate to have an abundance of recreation trails, state parks, nature preserves and wildlife sanctuaries. The creation of the Adirondack Park in 1892 and the Green Mountain National Forest in 1932 were important early conservation commitments that helped cultivate public appreciation for wilderness conservation and recovery, and they have encouraged the conservation of adjacent habitats. Over the last century, conservation groups, land trusts, landowners, voters and state and municipal governments have cooperated in protecting millions of acres for wild habitat and public access in the Champlain Valley. Outdoor recreation is one of the joys of living in the region, and it is increasingly recognized as a source of wellness and resilience for communities. With so many options, it is difficult to choose which trails to highlight. The following list provides a range of outdoor experiences across the length of Lake Champlain.

Ausable Chasm

Ausable Chasm is a two-mile-long sandstone gorge on the Ausable River, near the river's entrance to Lake Champlain. Located in Keeseville, New York, on the border of Essex and Clinton Counties, Ausable Chasm has been a tourist attraction since 1870 and has been dubbed "the Grand

Ausable Chasm's unique rock formations are wonderful to experience. *Library of Congress, public domain.*

Canyon of the Adirondacks." At the southern end of the gorge is Rainbow Falls, which is viewable from the Ausable Chasm bridge on Route 9 or from viewing platforms on the chasm trails. For a fee, various options are available to experience the canyon, waterfalls and river, including walking and hiking trails of varying difficulty, river tubing, rafting, rappelling and rock climbing.

SPLIT ROCK MOUNTAIN WILD FOREST

This 3,700-acre shoreline forest was saved from sale at auction in 1993, preserving the largest tract of undeveloped Lake Champlain shoreline in New York. Considered one of the lake's most scenic sections, it is located between Essex and Westport and includes Split Rock Mountain, Lake Champlain's highest peak. Towering more than 1,000 feet above the water with stunning views, Split Rock Mountain has cultural importance as a historic boundary point between the Algonquins and Iroquois and, later, between the French and English. The Split Rock Mountain Wild Forest includes 11 miles of hiking trails, rare habitats, waterfalls and the Lake Champlain Palisades, 150-foot sheer cliffs at lakeside. The site provides critical habitat for bald eagles and timber rattlesnakes. A range of activities are available, including hiking, birdwatching, paddling, boating, birding, snowshoeing, hunting, fishing and primitive camping.

MISSISQUOI NATIONAL WILDLIFE REFUGE

The Missisquoi National Wildlife Refuge was established in 1943 as a critical habitat for North American bird migration. Close to the United States–Canadian border in Swanton, Vermont, the 6,279-acre refuge is located on Missisquoi Bay at the mouth of the Missisquoi River and is part of the ancestral lands of the Abenaki. The refuge hosts more than two hundred bird species and is Vermont's only nesting site for endangered black terns, as well as bald eagles, osprey, herons, egrets and a variety of duck species. Although much of the refuge comprises wetlands, forests and grasslands are also maintained to protect endangered species, such as the bobolink and meadowlark and native pollinators. The river delta,

The trails of the Missisquoi National Wildlife Refuge are quiet, isolated and filled with natural beauty. *Photograph by Christine Eldred.*

bog and floodplains create a rich and diverse habitat for mammals and reptiles as well. The refuge has five walking trails, hunting and fishing areas and boating access. Trails are open to snowshoeing and cross-country skiing in winter.

SHELBURNE BAY PARK, LAPLATTE RIVER MARSH NATURAL AREA AND SHELBURNE FARMS

Shelburne, Vermont, provides evidence for the value of preserving natural sites in a more developed, suburban environment. Just west of busy Route 7 and Shelburne Village are three natural areas clustered close by, offering diverse habitats, peaceful walking trails and some of the best views on the lake. The LaPlatte River Marsh Natural Area is a 270-acre preserve of marsh and forest floodplain where the LaPlatte River meets Shelburne Bay. Providing essential habitats for birds, mammals and reptiles, the marsh also helps filter runoff from one of the most developed areas of the Champlain Valley. The natural area includes a 1.5-mile loop trail with views of the river, reclaimed farmland and marshland. Shelburne Bay Park is a 104-acre park with 4.7 miles of hiking and biking trails through forests and along the shore. A boat ramp provides access for watercraft, and the bay is a popular spot for paddling, sailing, fishing and watching the sunset over the Adirondacks. It is also known to host bald eagles, osprey and herons. To the west of the bay is Shelburne Farms, a unique location on Lake Champlain. The former estate and farm of the wealthy Webb family, Shelburne Farms is a national historic landmark, an educational nonprofit and a diversified working farm open to the public. The property was originally designed by landscape architect Frederick Law Olmstead and includes 10 miles of walking trails through beautiful gardens, open fields, pastures, orchards and lakeshore areas with fantastic views of the Green Mountains and Lake Champlain.

CROWN POINT STATE HISTORIC SITE

Located on a prominent point near a narrow section of Lake Champlain, Crown Point was strategically important to Natives, the French, the English and colonial Americans. The first fort here was built by the French in 1737. In 1759, the British captured the fort and built their own military installation, holding the site until the end of the American Revolution. Visitors can explore the ruins of the forts, visit the museum and enjoy walking trails around the battlefield site and Crown Point, crossing through fields and forests and along the lake. Other points of interest include the Champlain Memorial Lighthouse, a boat launch, a fishing pier, campgrounds and picnic sites.

17

What Lies Beneath

Shipwrecks

Some of the most interesting treasures in Lake Champlain are the vessels that rest at its bottom. There are far too many to detail in a single chapter. Even after extensive study, not every wreck has been documented, but a lot of information has been gathered about these hulks.

They are so close that they are almost tangible. They are quite accessible to historians and divers. With modern technology, they are becoming more accessible to the public.

Most of the lake is shared between New York and Vermont, and a sliver rests in Quebec. New York's underbelly contains approximately dozens of shipwrecks, at least two railroad cars, two valuable battlefield locations and the remains of the Ticonderoga and Mount Independence Bridge. The Vermont side, which was more developed, features scores shipwrecks, half of the historic bridge and cultural features indicating early Native settlement, including two pots dated to the Woodland period and dugout canoes.

Today, professional historians are doing what they can to preserve and protect these items. This has not always been the case. Private collectors have raided plenty of these historic sites. For years, people visited the wrecks like that of the *Royal Savage*, Benedict Arnold's vessel that sank off Valcour Island. The same happened to more of Arnold's ships that were abandoned near Vergennes. There are the War of 1812 vessels in Otter Creek.

Sometimes, early historians didn't get it quite right. The best example of changing professional and preservation ethics are the efforts of Lorenzo Haggland in 1932. He was interested in the remaining boards of the *Royal*

Savage. His work was done out in the open and was documented, but its result was far from today's standards. The historically priceless ship was disassembled, and collectors and museums preserved pieces of it.

Perhaps Haggland's most well-known recovery effort was that of the *Philadelphia*, another of Arnold's ships. Haggland returned to Valcour knowing the extent of the battle that was fought there. In 1935, his divers located the gunboat *Philadelphia* in about sixty feet of water. It was near the halfway point between the island and the New York shore. It had been untouched since October 1776. They worked to raise the vessel, which involved preservation efforts that were appropriate at the time. The ship was intact, and it was raised. It was displayed, an impressive symbol of the region's history. The *Philadelphia* toured in Vermont and New York. Haggland wasn't done. In the 1950s, he located and raised another Revolutionary War gunboat he found in Arnold's Bay. Officials in the Champlain Valley attempted to form a preservationist group, the Lake Champlain Associates, to maintain and display these vessels and artifacts. The effort fizzled, and much of Haggland's work was lost. In 1961, after Haggland passed away, the Smithsonian acquired the *Philadelphia* and added it to its collection. The critically important vessel is now on display for all Americans to see.

In 1909, the Fort Ticonderoga Museum investigated a shipwreck near the fort. It was below the old military dock that rested at water level on Lake Champlain. The vessel was eventually identified as the English warship the *Duke of Cumberland*, which was constructed in 1759 and used during the French and Indian War. The staff housed the hulk in a partially open shed. In 1948, its roof collapsed. There was significant damage to what was left of the old craft. The staff eventually left what remained alone, and it rotted on the lakeshore.

Two French sloops from the French and Indian War were scuttled around Cumberland Bay, near present-day Plattsburgh, in 1759. A somewhat public research and recovery effort unfolded in 1968, when three scuba divers found the exact location where the French had tried to destroy their ships. The divers recovered anchors, a sword, a swivel cannon and two bronze cannons. The State of New York contacted the divers and collected the two bronze canons. They are now on display at Crown Point. No one knows what happened to the other artifacts.

Another example of why historic preservation standards changed was what happened to another French and Indian War vessel, likely the *Grand Diable*. In the early 1900s, it was located and raised from the waters off from

Crown Point. It was put on display for travelers to see. However, this deed didn't keep the hull safe for future generations. Old wood, when underwater for long periods, tends to break down very quickly when brought to the surface. The hull of the *Grand Diable* was exposed to the elements and seasonal shifts in the weather. In the 1940s, a grass fire destroyed what was left. Nearly all the ships that have been recovered from the lake have been destroyed due to a disregard for long-term historic preservation.

Some of the efforts to let the public see a historic hulk were successful. In 1958, what was left of the schooner *Ticonderoga* was raised from its nautical graveyard in the Poultney River. It was brought to Whitehall, New York, and remains safe and largely intact in the Skenesborough Museum.

Not all the searches were successful. Another Revolutionary War boat, the British radeau *Thunderer*, was one of the most significant craft on the lake in the 1770s. It was effectively a floating arsenal, loaded with cannons and supplies. The British used her in campaigns in 1776 and 1777, but when the Saratoga Campaign failed, they retreated to Quebec. Historical documents suggest the worship sank somewhere off from Isle La Motte or Alburgh, but no evidence has ever been found.

A separate, more successful search was conducted in the lake's southern regions, and its finds were so great that they will be studied for years. The effort was conducted where the lake narrows considerably south of Fort Ticonderoga. This section of water was used extensively during the canal years, and preliminary work revealed at least twenty-two craft resting on its bottom. Most of these vessels are believed to be canal boats that were used during the economic booms of the 1800s. Because so many were used, canal boats represent, by far, most of the craft resting at the bottom of Lake Champlain.[329]

The effort to preserve underwater sites is as relevant as maintaining historic churches, old town greens and important battlefield locations. For years, with little concern or respect for preservation, people unknowingly destroyed, defaced or simply eliminated the nation's collective nautical history. By the 1980s and 1990s, historic preservation and documentation had vastly improved. Professionals and academics conducted surveys of the War of 1812 hulks that remained in the Poultney River, a canal sloop off the coast of Isle La Motte, a canal boat off Basin Harbor, the Mount Independence Bridge and the French and Indian War ships the *Duke of Cumberland* and the *Boscawen*. In 1983, the Lake Champlain Society dove and identified at least ten wrecks in Shelburne Bay. Historic accounts pointed to the possibility of at least thirteen there.

In 1996, the Lake Champlain Maritime Museum embarked on a long-term mission to catalogue and preserve what lies beneath. The museum was the prime mover in the Lake Champlain Underwater Cultural Resources Survey. It was a huge undertaking that had many participating groups. The group wanted to identify sites that had already been raided by amateurs and document the unknown shipwrecks and artifacts. It was like a local historical society striving to preserve what it could, but it had an entire lake to search.

Brochures, documents and online resources have been created. Laws have been passed that penalize overambitious divers and unscrupulous collectors for lifting artifacts from known archaeological sites. Those involved understand that the public must be involved in the underwater efforts. Obstructing public participation would be seen as elitist and hamper preservation.

There are also threats beyond those posed by people. Some of the larger shipwrecks have been disturbed when severe storms have passed above. Zebra mussels, a species that presents a threat when it latches onto underwater hulks in large numbers, arrived in the area decades ago. They are already damaging wreck sites. Quagga mussels haven't arrived yet but could do much more damage.[330]

The lake survey was conducted by the research vessel *Neptune*. It was equipped with a side scan sonar system, and Lake Champlain had never seen anything like it. The lead researcher, Arthur Cohen, and the research team settled on a forty-day research window. The *Neptune* operated between Plattsburgh and Cumberland Head on the New York side of the lake and went as far south as Shelburne Bay on the Vermont side. The *Neptune* explored about forty square miles, about 10 percent of the lake. A decision was made to go after sections that were most advantageous for research. In other words, if there was a hulk in twenty feet of water or less, it was accessible to divers and could be visited at some future date. The effort's primary focus was on deep-water wreck sites. It was broken down into two efforts. The first was the survey. The next was site identification. Middlebury College contributed greatly when it purchased an armored cable over nine hundred feet long that towed sonar equipment behind the *Neptune*. It was deployed in very deep waters and reeled in for shallower depths. The hope was to drag the sonar within sixteen to thirty feet along the lake bottom. The technology allowed for readings to be taken for about three hundred feet on either side of the device. Pings reflected off the shores, and the "hits" were recorded. It was very much like metal detectors scanning for coins or artifacts. The *Neptune* conducted over five hundred north–south tracts with the GPS receiver below the water. Even in 1996, the technology was good enough to record the depth and position of any new discovery. The researchers knew that this broad section of the lake had been extensively used over the centuries, even if many of the wrecks had already been located by historians or hobby divers. They hoped to confirm existing historical accounts and wanted to find unknown wreck sites.

The research uncovered over three hundred cultural and geological features. Ten were previously undiscovered shipwrecks. Unfortunately, five were in water deeper than 180 feet, too deep for the *Neptune*. The five others were under anywhere from 60 to 110 feet of water, depths achievable for professional divers. In August 1996, diving teams descended on these hulks and investigated.

Recording and cataloging involved significant organizational work. Areas of study were documented, locations were recorded and the *Neptune* moved on. The teams used the alphabet to identify every radar blip. Wrecks A, B and E were found on the New York side of the lake but were too deep for diver verification. Wrecks D, H and L were discovered in Vermont waters and were also too deep for divers. Wrecks C, F, G, I, J and K were all positively identified.

Wreck C was approximately eighty-five feet long and twelve feet wide. It rested upright on a sandy, level plane. When a diver investigated the site, it was confirmed to be a canal boat from the early 1900s in poor condition. Some of the boat had fallen apart. There appeared to be little or no cargo. It was learned that some local divers from Plattsburgh had visited this ship already, even though it had not been catalogued.

Wreck F was in Vermont waters, and diver examination revealed it was a sailing canal sloop still in very good condition. The vessel probably sank unexpectedly. The mast was still upright. The wood and some of the paint was in pristine condition. The cabin was a treasure-trove of artifacts that had remained in place. The survey team immediately recognized the wreck as a time capsule, as all the artifacts give clear indications about life on Lake Champlain during the mid-nineteenth century.

Local divers from New York were already aware of the depth and location of wreck G, but it was still important to survey it. The ship appears to have been a canal boat and may have been a type that was numerous. It is nearly one hundred feet long and about fifteen feet wide. The steering mechanism is still intact. The ship probably dates to the later portion of the nineteenth century.

A diver from the Lake Champlain Maritime Museum studies the wreck of the *Phoenix*. *Image Courtesy of the Lake Champlain Maritime Museum.*

The next wreck, I, was found in Shelburne Bay in the same general location as the previously mentioned vessel graveyard. It was a little longer than forty feet and was about twenty feet wide. The divers found it was a wooden tugboat with its steam-powered equipment still in place. Further research and historical accounts confirmed it was the *U.S. La Vallee*. It was scuttled in the 1930s. The boat's features have been very well preserved, including its propeller, steam stack and ship's wheel.

Wreck J was also in Vermont waters. It is about ninety-four feet long and about thirty feet wide. It was determined that it was a heavy wooden ship of a scow or barge design. Researchers believe it was a support construction vessel that worked on many of the docks along the shoreline communities. The team determined that it was probably intentionally scuttled based on its age. Some of the infrastructure design features unique to such craft were still in place, including the support timbers meant to hold large deck loads. This type of wooden craft was replaced by steel barges, suggesting this vessel was used in the early 1800s.

Wreck K was previously known, as it had been discovered in Vermont waters back in 1983. It was determined that it was a sloop-rigged sailing canal boat.

Of the wrecks that were discovered and documented by divers, the *U.S. La Vallee* was the most solid confirmation and provided the most complete story. Since it had been positively identified, its story could be told. This begged the question: Would it be possible to research other vessels and find similar histories? In 1880, a tiny wood tugboat was built in Brooklyn, New York. Its name was *Henry Lloyd*. The ship was a coal-fired steamer that was common to the era, and it would have worked the coastal waters of the Atlantic. Over the years, the vessel's license changed hands, as it was totally rebuilt in 1907. It was moved to work the coastal waters off South Carolina, where it spent most of its years. Around 1923, the *Henry Lloyd*'s named was changed to the *U.S. La Vallee*, and it did more work in the New York area. Around 1929, the tug was sold yet again, this time to someone with connections in Burlington and on Lake Champlain. For months, there were efforts to repair and fix the many leaks in the now-fifty-year-old craft. However, with the Depression and the changing uses of Lake Champlain, the owners had little use for the vessel.

It was sunk on June 12, 1931, and researchers have pieced together what happened when it was discarded. The wheelhouse was in multiple pieces, as though it had been blown outward. This might be where a detonation occurred, just prior to it joining the rest of the hulks at the bottom of the lake. It is still in good condition at the bottom of Shelburne Bay.

The 250th anniversary of the Revolutionary War is fast approaching. One of the most significant wrecks in Lake Champlain comes from that conflict. The *Spitfire*, another of Benedict Arnold's ships, sank during the retreat from Valcour Island. It had been missing for over a century. Historians were aware that the gunboat was critically damaged during the cannon exchanges with the British fleet. It was limping along, trying to stay ahead of the enemy. Until recently, the only information about the location of the *Spitfire* came from the accounts of Arnold's men, as recorded in field reports and journals. Well into the 1990s, historians still did not know where the wreck was—or if it was even there.

But recently, during the second year of the lake survey, its location was discovered. The vessel was perfectly preserved, virtually untouched. Historians salivated and researchers itched to uncover its secrets. It measured about fifty-four feet long, showcasing the same design as that of the other boats in Arnold's fleet. Its bow cannon was still in place. The *Spitfire*'s mast was still erect, standing firm like any flagpole commemorating a critical American battlefield.

The *Spitfire*'s rediscovery presents huge issues for preservationists, historians, teachers and the public. The very same problems that plagued wrecks through the 1900s continue today. If unscrupulous private divers became aware of its exact location, would they go looking for relics? The management of the *Spitfire* is a huge issue, considering the zebra and quagga mussel threat. While the historically priceless boat rests at the lake bottom, it is well preserved by the cold, fresh water. There is little or no evidence that the mussels have latched on, so the ship's short-term safety is not in peril. However, if a clear and present danger emerges, there are huge questions to be answered. Raising the vessel would cost somewhere in the range of $60 million. That price tag might seem high, but the money would be well spent. The ship would be safely brought up intact, and then the appropriate sealants would be applied to prevent decay. Then longer term issues would arise. Where would the *Spitfire* be stored? How would it be maintained? The answers to these questions only add to the costs. Patriotism and respect can be strong motivators, and the *Spitfire* may become an uplifting character in American history. American soldiers fought and died on the vessels of Arnold's fleet, and this may elevate the ship to a worthy level of reverence. Hopefully the threats can be avoided, and the vessel can remain quietly preserved.

All of this information comes from the first years of the Lake Champlain survey.

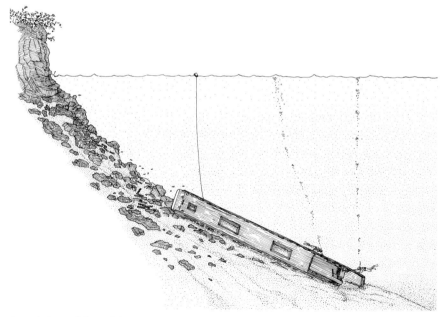

An artist's rendition of the state of the *Stove Wreck*, resting at the bottom of Lake Champlain. *Image Courtesy of the Lake Champlain Maritime Museum.*

The work continued for years.

After the War of 1812, the surviving naval vessels from that war served on the lake. Two of the vessels in the fleet were the former British frigate *Confiance* and the British sloop *Linnet*. The others were the American ships *Ticonderoga*, *Eagle* and *Saratoga*; five smaller sloops; and ten gunboats. In 1815, the smaller sloops and the gunboats were stripped of their armaments and sold into private service. Five of the gunboats were sunk in the narrow channel of the lake, just north of Whitehall. The final gunboat, the *Allen*, was kept in service for a few years. The larger vessels were stripped of much of their equipment and rigging. By 1820, the U.S. government had moved them to the mouth of the Poultney River, as they were already rotting. They were sold off, but the hulks were just allowed to sink.

Sadly, the fate of the *Confiance* is very similar to that of any household item thrown away in the trash. When its hulk and frame sank, it was just left alone. In 1824, part of the hull was apparently dismantled, but enough of it remained to be noted on an 1839 map of the mouth of the Poultney River. Despite several dives and professional archaeological surveys of that section of the lake, it appears the largest warship to ever sail on Lake Champlain no longer exits.

The final fate of the rest of the fleet is just as interesting. The *Ticonderoga* was removed from the ship graveyard by the Town of Whitehall and was part of a historical display for the town. No preservation techniques were deployed. When the display was completed, it was given to the Skenesborough Museum, where it is still on display, partially preserved. The rest of the 1812 fleet still lies at the mouth of the Poultney River, and a significant study has been conducted. Much of the *Eagle* remains underwater and is partially preserved. The *Allen*, the gunboat that remained in service for a decade after the War of 1812, also ended up discarded in the river. It rests not far from the *Eagle*. The final vessel, the *Linnet*, was partially removed and damaged in 1949 when a local landowner attempted to drag the ship out of the water with horses and three tractors. A portion broke off and floated down the river, never to be seen again. What little remained of the vessel slipped back into the Poultney River.[331]

A sampling of the other wrecks provides a tantalizing history of the lake.

In 1999, when the Cultural Resources Survey focused on the south-central portion of Champlain, Wreck OO was discovered. Not much is known about it, as it was identified in two hundred feet of water. Resting on the bottom of the lake for well over one hundred years, the ship was obscured by silt sediment and lake weeds. Only about twelve inches of its hull was exposed. The frame was rectangular, denoting that it very likely was a lake barge. Most of the hull appeared to have been made of substantial pieces of timber, although there appeared to be ironwork supporting the frame.[332]

The northern edges of the lake, while shallow, also hosted plenty of underwater secrets. Although it was a previously known wreck, a vessel lies approximately ten feet underwater just off the Rouses Point and Windmill Point trestle bridge. Its location and general construction suggest that it was probably one of the barges used to maintain the train bridge. Identified as the Rouses Point Barge, or wreck WW, it is one hundred feet long and thirty feet wide. There is no cargo on the main deck, indicating the ship was discarded and sunk. Examination of the hull revealed that it was likely built after the completion of the Champlain Bridge Canal in 1916.[333] The design suggests it was used to transport bulk cargo, likely iron ore, coal or stone. The currents at the northern end of the lake present issues for future study. However, most wrecks are far deeper, so the Rouses Point Barge is a rare find.

Even more accessible is the lake barge resting off the coast of Grand Isle. This is a modern craft, probably used in the middle of the twentieth century, and it sits just below the surface. In the spring, it is partially submerged due to high water and spring runoff. During the summer, as the lake level generally lowers, the upper sections of the wreck become exposed. It is approximately fifty feet long and fifteen feet wide. At one point, it was used as a dock by a nearby property owner. Even with the modern origins of this vessel, not much about it is known. It was catalogued as wreck FFF.[334]

One of the more interesting ships on the lake's bottom may be the Port Henry Draw Boat. It is probably the lake's largest wreck and lies in only 10 feet of water.[335] This craft's function was intimately linked to the railroads. It was a floating railroad connector, linking the two bridges from the shores. It could be moved out of the way so that other boats could move north and south, unencumbered by the tracks and trestles. When trains approached on a fixed schedule, this boat was moved back into place. The deck had two different sets of tracks. The Port Henry Draw Boat was used mostly by local business interests, as it connected the iron ore from Port Henry to the furnaces located in Crown Point. A lot of work and engineering went into this project, and it was used during the 1871 mining season. In the winter of 1871–72, the small railroad trestles were damaged by ice, and the overall project was deemed too expensive to repair. The 250-foot-long deck was stripped of its rails prior to it being scuttled. It is generally still in excellent condition. This draw boat offers a glimpse into what transportation looked like over the other rail bridges on Lake Champlain.

Another part of the lake's economic is history is captured with the brick barge (Wreck GGG), located in Mallett's Bay, near Colchester, Vermont. This area is highly traveled by recreational craft, and the vessel rests about twenty feet below the surface. It is relatively small, measuring approximately twenty-five feet long. This wreck sank almost fully loaded with bricks. Its design suggests a late nineteenth- or early twentieth-century construction and that the local economy featured brick making. Further study could reveal a lot more about the region's local history.

One of the lake's most unique craft lies in Burlington Bay. It was a horse ferry and shows how animals were briefly used to power ships prior to the development of steam, coal or more modern forms of fuel. The craft is sixty-three feet long and twenty-three feet wide, and its most enticing features, two large propulsion turn-wheels, are still intact.[336] This delicate vessel is still in good condition, and divers have determined where the workhorses were used. It is under approximately fifty feet of water, and historians are hoping further research will reveal more about this vessel.

Also located in Burlington Bay, right near the breakwater and under about forty feet of water, is the *General Butler*. Historians know a lot about this vessel, as its history has been extensively researched; it is also a common destination for local divers. The *General Butler* sank in December 1876, when a winter stormed moved in. It was repeatedly thrust against the breakwater, successive powerful waves throwing the sailing canal boat against the rocks. Its captain and crew escaped, but the vessel sank. It was eighty-five feet long and fourteen feet wide.[337]

One of the most well-known wrecks rests on the New York side of the lake, just north of Westport, New York. It is the lake steamer *Champlain II*, and it has garnered considerable attention. Its steamship status has made it the focus of a significant research over the years. It was originally named the *Oaks Ames* and was launched in 1868. It was renamed the *Champlain II* in 1874, and it sank the next year. There was a crew shift change, and there is considerable evidence that the new captain may have been on morphine at the time of the accident. The ship ran aground at Barn Rock.[338] The company that owned the ship tried to salvage some portions of it, but it slid into the lake and now rests under approximately 20 to 30 feet of water. A large section of the ships 250-foot-long hull remains.

Efforts have been made to preserve and promote some of the shipwrecks. Five have been listed in the National Register of Historic Places; for the

Empire State, these include the *Champlain II*, and on the Vermont side, there are four sunken vessels: the *Phoenix*, the Burlington Bay Horse Ferry, the sailing schooner *O.J. Walker* and the *General Butler*. As historic perseveration became more academic and professional, the Lake Champlain Maritime Museum developed programming to attract hobby divers. It arranged some of the first field schools, where divers could visit, experience and enjoy some of the ship remains.

There are plenty of treasures at the bottom of Lake Champlain. Most of them will never be visited. Technology has developed greatly since the initial lake surveys, and historians, preservationists and educators are working together to make these wrecks available to the public. Long ago, those from Vermont and New York had to use their imaginations to visualize what lay beneath Lake Champlain. A few decades ago, sonar technology brought the mysteries of the deep into the public sphere. Now, technology is improving by leaps and bounds, and the internet allows people at home to access 3D images of some of these wrecks. It is a marvelous time to be interested in Lake Champlain's history.

NOTES

Chapter 1

1. Hallowell, "Story of Lake Champlain," 63–67.
2. Ibid.
3. Albers, *Hands on the Land*, 36.
4. Hallowell, "Story of Lake Champlain," 64–67.
5. Albers, *Hands on the Land*, 45–47.
6. Hallowell, "Story of Lake Champlain," 65–67.
7. Sherman, Sessions and Potash, *Freedom and Unity*, 9–10.
8. Ibid., 14.
9. Wiseman, *Seven Sisters*, 60, 118, 146–70.
10. Albers, *Hands on the Land*, 39–44.
11. Bellico, *Chronicles of Lake Champlain*, 36.
12. Rogers, "History Space."

Chapter 2

13. Sherman, Sessions and Potash, *Freedom and Unity*, 33.
14. Albers, *Hands on the Land*, 69.
15. Ibid., 65–66.
16. Sherman, Sessions and Potash, *Freedom and Unity*, 40.
17. Ibid., 44.

18. Coolidge, *French Occupation of the Champlain Valley*, 82–84.
19. Albers, *Hands on the Land*, 44–46.
20. Ibid., 46
21. Sherman, Sessions and Potash, *Freedom and Unity*, 59.
22. Albers, *Hands on the Land*, 76.
23. Sherman, Sessions and Potash, *Freedom and Unity*, 60.
24. Ibid.
25. Albers, *Hands on the Land*, 76.
26. Coolidge, *French Occupation of the Champlain Valley*, 100–4.
27. Ibid., 94.
28. Ibid., 95.
29. Sherman, Sessions and Potash, *Freedom and Unity*, 56.
30. Coolidge, *French Occupation of the Champlain Valley*, 121.
31. Ibid., 164.
32. Sherman, Sessions and Potash, *Freedom and Unity*, 63.

Chapter 3

33. Wickman, *Strong Ground*, 50.

Chapter 4

34. Coolidge, *French Occupation of the Champlain Valley*, 30.
35. Ibid., 29–31.
36. Sayers, "Saint Anne's Shrine."
37. Coolidge, *French Occupation of the Champlain Valley*, 37–44.
38. Saint Anne's Shrine, "Our History."

Chapter 6

39. Bellico, *Sail and Steam*, 216.
40. Ibid., 261.
41. Ibid., 263.
42. FreightWaves.
43. Hamilton College, "Commercial Era of the 1800s."
44. Ibid.

45. Ibid.

46. Texas A&M University, "Canal Boat Wrecks of Lake Champlain."

47. Ibid.

48. Crisman, "Vermont's Steamboat Pioneer," 120–24.

49. Ibid.

50. Bellico, *Sail and Steam*, 263.

51. Ibid., 266.

52. Crisman, "Vermont's Steamboat Pioneer," 124.

53. Ibid.

54. FreightWaves.

55. Burlington Vermont: Early 20th Century Postcard Views.

56. Champlain History Center, "Canal Boat Industry in the Village."

57. FreightWaves.

58. Bellico, *Sail and Steam*, 269.

59. Kingsley and Ronald Astmann, "Burleigh Brothers."

60. Champlain History Center, "Canal Boat Industry in the Village."

61. Hamilton College, "Commercial Era of the 1800s."

62. Ibid.

63. UVM Landscape Change Program.

64. Kingsley and Ronald Astmann, "Burleigh Brothers."

65. Bellico, *Sail and Steam*, 270.

66. Vermont Historical Society, "Researching Lake Champlain Celebrations."

67. FreightWaves.

68. Burlington Vermont: Early 20th Century Postcard Views.

69. Vermont Historical Society, "Researching Lake Champlain Celebrations."

70. Bellico, *Sail and Steam*, 281.

Chapter 7

71. "Painsville and Campbellburgh," *Saint Albans Daily Messenger*.

72. "Vermont and Canada Railroad," *Burlington Free Press*.

73. "Northern Railroad," *Plattsburgh Republican*.

74. "Visit of the Vermont Legislature," *Saint Albans Weekly Messenger*.

75. "Bridge at Rouses Point," *Saint Albans Weekly Messenger*.

76. "Vermont Railroads," *Spirit of the Age*.

77. "The Line of Boats," *Plattsburgh Republican*.

78. "Central Vermont Railroad!" *Saint Albans Weekly Messenger*.

79. Jones, *Railroads of Vermont Volume I*, 176.

80. Ibid., 74, 151.
81. "State Matters," *Daily Journal.*
82. "Addison County Railroad," *Rutland Daily Herald.*
83. "Town Meeting," *Middlebury Register.*
84. "Addison County," *Vermont Standard.*
85. "Addison Railroad," *Rutland Daily Herald,* November 7, 1870.
86. "Two Men Buried Alive," *Rutland Weekly Herald.*
87. "Ticonderoga Bridge," *Rutland Weekly Herald.*
88. "The Manufacture and Builder," *Vermont Watchman and State Journal.*
89. "New Railroad Projects," *Rutland Weekly Herald.*
90. "Killed," *Burlington Free Press.*
91. "State at Large," *Spirit of the Age,* April 27, 1871.
92. "Addison County," *Middlebury Register,* May 2, 1871.
93. "Middlebury," *Rutland Daily Globe.*
94. "Addison Railroad," *Rutland Daily Globe,* September 27, 1871.
95. "Addison County," *Middlebury Register,* November 28, 1871.
96. "Operated from Rutland," *Vermont Phoenix.*
97. "Over the State," *Enterprise and Vermonter.*
98. "Our New Road," *Burlington Daily News.*
99. "Rutland-Canadian R.R.," *Vermont Phoenix,* April 7, 1899, 3.
100. "The Rutland-Canadian," *Burlington Free Press,* April 12, 1899, 6.
101. "State of Vermont," *News and Advertiser,* May 16, 1899.
102. "Grand Isle," *Burlington Free Press,* June 7, 1899, 7.
103. "South Hero," *Swanton Courier,* June 15, 1899, 4.
104. "Earth," *Burlington Local News,* July 29, 1899, 8.
105. "News of the State," *Burlington Clipper.*
106. "Grand Isle," *Earth.*
107. "A Glance Over the State," *Middlebury Register,* November 24, 1899.
108. "Vermont News Items," *Montpelier Evening Argus,* 2.
109. "Local News Items," *Plattsburgh Daily Press,* November 17, 1899, 6.
110. "Paragrams," *Plattsburgh Sentinel,* December 22, 1899, 1.
111. "Grand Isle," *Saint Albans Daily Messenger,* December 20, 1899.
112. "Vermont News Items," *Montpelier Evening Argus.*
113. "Rutland Wins," *Middlebury Register.*
114. "Colchester," *Burlington Clipper,* January 27, 1900.
115. "South Hero," *Burlington Free Press.*
116. "Glance Over the State," *Middlebury Register.*
117. "Mr. Editor," *Burlington Clipper.*
118. "Italian Quarrel," *Burlington Free Press.*

119. "State of Vermont," *Landmark*.
120. "Grand Isle," *Saint Albans Daily Messenger*.
121. Ibid.
122. "Stepped Out Too Soon," *Saint Albans Messenger*.
123. "Injured by Blast," *Burlington Free Press*.

Chapter 8

124. Adirondack Architectural Heritage, "Architecture of the Champlain Valley."
125. Uhl, "Recollections of Westport Inn."
126. Aldrich, *History of Franklin and Grand Isle Counties*, 623–24.
127. Sheldon Historical Society, "The Springs."
128. Williams, *Adirondack Hotels and Inns*, 114.
129. "Hotel Ausable Open," *Lake Placid News*, 14; "Masonic Convention," *Elizabethtown Post*, 1.
130. Swanton Historical Society, "Outline of Swanton's History."
131. "About Town," *Swanton Courier*, 3.
132. "Original Hotel Champlain," *Swanton Courier*, 8.
133. Preservation Trust of Vermont, "1903–1956: The Island Villa Hotel."
134. "About Town," *Swanton Courier*, 1.
135. Swanton Historical Society, "Outline of Swanton's History."
136. "Day at Missisquoi Park," *Saint Albans Daily Messenger*, 3.
137. Payne, "Memorial: Orlando Kellog Jr."
138. "Windsor and Cottages," *Brooklyn Daily Eagle*, 44.
139. Adirondack History Museum, Facebook post and comment.

Chapter 9

140. Rowe, *God's Strange Work*, 37.
141. Ibid., 8.
142. Ibid., 15–16.
143. Ibid., 40–41.
144. Ibid., 70–71.
145. Ibid., 73.
146. Ibid., 81.
147. Ibid., 75.

148. Bliss, *Memoirs*, 82.
149. Rowe, *God's Strange Work*, 95.
150. Ibid., 98
151. Bliss, *Memoirs*, 99.
152. Rowe, *God's Strange Work*, 103.
153. Bliss, *Memoirs*, 112.
154. Ibid., 118.
155. Ibid., 122.
156. "Millerism vs Abolitionism," *Universalist Watchman*.
157. "A Millerite," *Sentinel and Democrat*.
158. "Question Answered," *Universalist Watchman*.
159. "A Good Joke," *Spirit of the Age*.
160. "Daily Number of Attendees," *Vermont Statesman*.
161. *Plattsburgh Republican*, September 10, 1842, 3.
162. "Millerism," *Middlebury People's Press*.
163. "Monthly Mis. of Religion and Letters," *Vermont Phoenix*.
164. "Imposters," *Middlebury People's Press*.
165. "Millerism," *Vermont Patriot and State Gazette*.
166. "Insanity by Millerism," *Universalist Watchman*.
167. "*Boston Post* Says," *New York Tribune*.
168. "Millerites," *Middlebury People's Press*.
169. "Good Fruits," *North Star*.
170. "A Singular Phenomenon," *Vermont Mercury*.
171. "Signs of the 2nd Coming," *Universalist Watchmen*.
172. Ibid.
173. "Another Sign," *Vermont Religious Observer*.
174. Miller to Himes, February 4, 1844.
175. Knight, *Search for Identity*, n.p.
176. Bliss, *Memoirs*, n.p.

Chapter 10

177. "President's Vacation," *Brooklyn Citizen*.
178. "McKinley's Vacation," *Brooklyn Daily Eagle*, July 15, 1897.
179. "Notes," *Brooklyn Daily Eagle*.
180. "At Hotel Champlain," *Star Gazette*.
181. "President's Summer Home," *New York Times*.
182. "McKinley Resting," *Buffalo Commercial*.

183. "President's Holiday," *Buffalo Morning Express*.
184. "President's Rest," *New York Tribune*.
185. "President's Outing," *New York Tribune*.
186. Ibid.
187. "McKinley's Sunday," *Democrat and Chronicle*.
188. "President's Sunday," *New York Tribune*.
189. "Delightful Day," *Democrat and Chronicle*.
190. Ibid.
191. "Pass in Review," *Standard Union*.
192. "Delightful Day," *Democrat and Chronicle*.
193. "Hobart Joins McKinley," *World*.
194. "McKinley in Vermont," *World*.
195. "President McKinley in Vermont," *Buffalo News*.
196. "McKinley in Burlington," *Brooklyn Daily Eagle*.
197. "Visited Fort Ethan Allen," *Hornellsville Weekly Tribune*.
198. "Cheers for the President," *New York Tribune*.
199. "McKinley to Be Guest," *Brooklyn Daily Eagle*.
200. "President's Outing," *New York Tribune*.
201. "President Horrified," *New York Times*.
202. "President at the Garrison," *Democrat and Chronicle*.
203. "McKinley to Summer," *Yonkers Herald*.
204. "McKinley's Vacation," *Brooklyn Daily Eagle*, July 27, 1899.
205. "Hereaux's Death Confirmed," *Standard Union*.
206. "Mrs. McKinley Much Better," *Democrat and Chronicle*.
207. "President's Sunday," *New York Tribune*.
208. "McKinley's Vacation," *Brooklyn Daily Eagle*, July 27, 1899.
209. "McKinley's Guests," *Star Gazette*.
210. "President Dodging Kodaks," *Brooklyn Citizen*.
211. "President's Rest," *New York Tribune*.
212. "Abner Visits His Brother," *Brooklyn Citizen*.
213. "At the Champlain Hotel," *Buffalo News*.
214. "Vice President Hobart Ill," *Standard Union*.
215. "Callers on the President," *Standard Union*.
216. "No Backdown," *Buffalo Commercial*.
217. "Rain and Cold Weather," *Brooklyn Citizen*.
218. "McKinley's Vacation," *Brooklyn Daily Eagle*, July 27, 1899.
219. "McKinley Says No," *Buffalo Times*.
220. "McKinley's Vacation," *Brooklyn Daily Eagle*, July 27, 1899.
221. "*New York Times* Illustrated Magazine," *New York Times*.

222. "President Goes Yachting," *Buffalo Times*.
223. "Day of Pleasure," *Yonkers Herald*.
224. "McKinley Invited," *Standard Union*.
225. "The Flag," *Buffalo Commercial*.
226. *Brooklyn Life*, August 19, 1899.
227. "What Is Doing in Society," *New York Times*.
228. "Mrs. McKinley Better," *Democrat and Chronicle*.
229. "President Reviews Troops," *New York Times*.
230. "President Spending a Quiet Day," *Brooklyn Citizen*.
231. "Lake Champlain," *Plattsburgh Republican*, August 1899.
232. "Will Be in Buffalo Today," *Buffalo Morning Express*.
233. "Secretary Root with McKinley," *Buffalo Inquirer*.
234. "Root Goes to Plattsburgh," *New York Times*.
235. "Last of Summer School," *Catholic Union and Times*.
236. "Latest News," *Buffalo News*.
237. "Timely Topics," *Buffalo Review*.
238. "Vacation Ended," *Buffalo News*.

Chapter 11

239. "Advanced Spiritualism and Free Love," *Buffalo Evening Post*.
240. "Strange Piece of News," *Burlington Free Press*.
241. "Free Lovers," *New York Daily Herald*.
242. "New Free Love Enterprise," *Burlington Weekly Free Press*.
243. "Dawn Valcour Community," *Burlington Free Press*.
244. Ibid.
245. "Colchester," *Burlington Free Press*.
246. "*Herald* Correspondent," *Burlington Free Press*.
247. "State at Large," *Vermont Standard*, October 1, 1874.
248. "Free Conferences," *Saint Albans Daily Messenger*.
249. "Dawn," *Burlington Daily Sentinel*.
250. "Brief Mention," *Burlington Daily Sentinel*.
251. "Valcourians," *New York Daily Herald*.
252. "More Social Madness," *New York Daily Herald*.
253. "Vermont Notes," *Rutland Daily Globe*.
254. "Colonel Wilcox," *Burlington Free Press*.
255. "St. Albans and Vicinity," *Saint Albans Daily Messenger*.
256. "Dawn Valcour Community," *Burlington Free Press*.

257. "Dawn Valcour Community," *Rutland Daily Globe.*
258. "Communication from Mr. Shipman," *Burlington Free Press.*
259. "Vermont Utah," *News and Citizen.*
260. *Argus and Patriot*, February 18, 1875.
261. "State at Large," *Vermont Standard*, February 18, 1875.
262. "Over the Lake," *Saint Albans Daily Messenger.*
263. "Vermont Notes," *Rutland Daily Globe.*
264. "Dawn Valcour Community," *Rutland Daily Globe.*
265. "Colonel Wilcox," *Burlington Free Press.*
266. "Dawn Valcour Community," *News and Citizen.*
267. "Valcour Difficulty," *Rutland Daily Globe.*
268. "Mrs. Oren Shipman," *Woodstock Post.*
269. "Dawn Valcour Community," *News and Citizen.*
270. "Dawn Valcour Community," *Democrat and Weekly Sentinel.*
271. "Shipman vs. Wilcox and White," *Burlington Daily Sentinel.*
272. "Dawn Valcour Community," *Burlington Free Press.*
273. "End of the Dawn Valcour Community," *Saint Albans Daily Messenger.*
274. "Chittenden County," *Vermont Watchman and State Journal.*
275. "End of the Dawn Valcour Community," *Saint Albans Daily Messenger.*
276. "Good Bye, Valcour," *Rutland Daily Globe.*
277. "St. Albans and Vicinity," *Saint Albans Daily Messenger.*

Chapter 12

278. Bellico, *Chronicles of Lake Champlain*, 277.
279. Adirondack Architectural Heritage, "Architecture of the Champlain Valley."
280. Founders Online, "Thomas Jefferson to Martha Jefferson Randolph."
281. Crisman, "Vermont's Steamboat Pioneer."
282. O'Connor, "Hail to the Chiefs."
283. Bellico, *Sail and Steam*, 267.
284. Ibid., 272.
285. "President Arrives," *Montpelier Evening Argus.*
286. O'Connor, "Hail to the Chiefs."
287. "Roosevelt the Guest of Honor," *Saint Albans Daily Messenger.*
288. "Fish and Game League," *Vermont Phoenix.*
289. "President Coming to Vermont," *Burlington Free Press.*
290. "President Here," *Burlington Free Press.*

291. Ibid.
292. "Narrow Escape," *Burlington Free Press*.
293. Champlain History Center, "Canal Boat Industry in the Village."
294. Bellico, *Sail and Steam*, 282.
295. "Roosevelt the Guest of Honor," *Saint Albans Daily Messenger*.

Chapter 13

296. University of Vermont Silver Special Collections Library, "Queen City Park Association Records."
297. Mazowita, "Red Rocks Park," 3–5.
298. Blanchard-O'Brien, "History Space: Vermont's Mediums and Spirits."
299. "Spiritualist Camp Meeting," *North Star*.
300. "Remembering Queen City Park," *Burlington Free Press*.
301. Schneider, "Looking Back."
302. "Queen City Park," *Burlington Clipper*.
303. University of Vermont Silver Special Collections Library, "Queen City Park Association Records."
304. "Fire Destroys 13 Queen City Park Buildings," *Burlington Free Press and Times*.
305. University of Vermont Silver Special Collections Library, "Queen City Park Association Records."

Chapter 14

306. "Smuggling in Liquor," *Brattleboro Daily Reformer*.
307. "Vermont News," *Brattleboro Daily Reformer*, December 26, 1922.
308. "Vermont News," *Brattleboro Daily Reformer*, November 20, 1922.
309. "Motorboat Patrol on Lake Champlain," *Burlington Free Press*, 1.
310. "U.S. Officers Face Problem," *Plattsburgh Sentinel*.
311. "Barge of Hay Being Held," *Plattsburgh Sentinel*, 6.
312. "Seize Rowboat," *Ticonderoga Sentinel*, 2.
313. "Seize Five Booze Cars," *Plattsburgh Republican*.
314. "Lake Patrol Seize Yacht," *Plattsburgh Republican*.
315. "Close Navigation," *Ticonderoga Sentinel*.
316. "Babcock's Body Still in the Lake," *Plattsburgh Republican*.
317. "Babcock's Body Still Not Recovered," *Plattsburgh Republican*.
318. "Officer While Fishing Spots Ale Laden Boat," *Plattsburgh Republican*.

319. "Willsboro Man Caught," *Plattsburgh Republican.*
320. "Lake Patrol Seize Two Motor Boats," *Plattsburgh Daily Press.*
321. "Supposed Rum Runner Found," *Burlington Free Press*, 6.
322. "Rumrunner Knocks into Lake," *Plattsburgh Republican*, 3.
323. "Rum Boat Has Not Yet Been Found," *Plattsburgh Republican*, 3.
324. "Supposed Rum Boat Is Found," *Plattsburgh Republican*, 3.
325. "1,000 Cases of Ale Seized," *Plattsburgh Republican*, 3.

Chapter 15

326. "Finds Big Cannonball," *Swanton Courier*, 1.
327. National Weather Service, "Lake Champlain Extremes and Level."
328. "May Be Bunker Hill Gun," *Saint Albans Daily Messenger.*

Chapter 17

329. Texas A&M University, "The Canal Boat Wrecks of Lake Champlain."
330. Kane and Sabick, "Lake Champlain Underwater Cultural Resources Survey."
331. Lake Champlain Maritime Museum, "War of 1812 Wrecks."
332. Kane and Sabick, "Wreck OO."
333. Lake Champlain Maritime Museum, "Wreck WW."
334. Kane, Sabick and Brigadier, "Wreck FFF."
335. Kane and Sabick, "Port Henry Drawboat."
336. Lake Champlain Maritime Museum, "Horse Ferry."
337. Lake Champlain Maritime Museum, "Shipwreck Tour: *General Butler.*"
338. Lake Champlain Maritime Museum, "Steamboat *Champlain II.*"

BIBLIOGRAPHY

Adirondack Architectural Heritage. "Architecture of the Champlain Valley: Wadhams and Westport." Lakes to Locks Passage. https://passageport. org/wp-content/uploads/2020/11/wadhamswestport.pdf.

Adirondack History Museum. Facebook post and comment. March 25, 2015. https://www.facebook.com/AdkHistoryMuseum/photos/the-windsor-hotel-in-elizabethtown-ny/10152621069670146/.

Albers, Jan. *Hands on the Land: A History of the Vermont Landscape*. Cambridge, MA: MIT Press for the Orton Family Foundation, 2000.

Aldrich, Lewis Cass. *History of Franklin and Grand Isle Counties, Vermont: With Illustrations and Biographical Sketches of Some of the Prominent Men and Pioneers*. Syracuse, NY: Mason & Co., 1891.

Argus and Patriot. February 18, 1875. 2.

Bellico, Russell P. *Chronicles of Lake Champlain: Journeys in War and Peace*. Fleischmanns, NY: Purple Mountain Press, 1999.

———. *Sail and Steam in the Mountains*. Freichmann, NY: Purple Mountain Press, 1992.

Blanchard-O'Brien, Sally. "History Space: Vermont's Mediums and Spirits." *Burlington Free Press*, October 28, 2017. https://www.burlingtonfreepress. com/story/news/2017/10/28/history-space-vermonts-mediums-spirits/107113274/.

Bliss, Sylvester. *Memoirs of William Miller*. Boston, MA: Joshua Himes, 1853.

Brattleboro Daily Reformer. "Smuggling in Liquor." August 22, 1922.

———. "Vermont News." December 26, 1922.

———. "Vermont News." November 20, 1922.

Brooklyn Citizen. "Abner Visits His Brother." August 4, 1899, 10.

———. "McKinley Out Driving." August 5, 1899, 12.

———. "McKinley Will Leave Washington Wednesday." July 26, 1897, 2.

———. "President Dodging Kodaks." August 2, 1899, 9.

———. "The President Spending a Quiet Day." August 20, 1899, 7.

———. "The President's Vacation." July 9, 1897, 2.

———. "Rain and Cold Weather Mar President's Visit." August 10, 1899, 12.

———. "Reviewed by the President." August 2, 1897, 2.

Brooklyn Daily Eagle. "At the Hotel Champlain." August 16, 1899, 5.

———. "Lake Champlain." August 20, 1899, 32.

———. "McKinley in Burlington." August 4, 1897, 1.

———. "McKinley's Vacation." July 15, 1897, 7.

———. "McKinley's Vacation." July 27, 1899, 3.

———. "McKinley to Be Guest." August 6, 1897, 1.

———. "Notes." July 24, 1897, 10.

———. "The Windsor and Cottages, Elizabethtown, New York, Now Open." June 4, 1916, 44.

Brooklyn Life. August 19, 1899, 13.

Buffalo Commercial. "'The Flag' His Subject." August 16, 1899, 2.

———. "McKinley Resting." July 30, 1897, 2.

———. "No Backdown on War Policy." August 9, 1899, 2.

———. "Personal." September 24, 1874.

———. "Reviewed by the President." August 3, 1897, 1.

Buffalo Evening Post. "Advanced Spiritualism and Free Love to Be Its Distinguishing Characteristics." September 10, 1874, 2.

Buffalo Inquirer. "Secretary Root with McKinley." August 22, 1899, 8.

Buffalo Morning Express. "President's Holiday." July 31, 1897, 1.

———. "Will Be in Buffalo Today." August 17, 1899, 1.

Buffalo News. "At the Champlain Hotel." August 7, 1899, 5.

———. "Latest News by the Wire." August 24, 1899, 4.

———. "President McKinley in Vermont." August 4, 1897, 1.

———. "President's Sunday." July 31, 1899, 4.

———. "Vacation Ended." August 25, 1899, 5.

Buffalo Review. "Off for Long Branch." August 26, 1899, 2.

———. "Timely Topics." September 6, 1899, 4.

Buffalo Times. "McKinley Says No." August 13, 1899.

———. "President Goes Yachting with Mrs. McKinley." August 14, 1899, 1.

———. "Secretary Root Join McKinley." August 22, 1899, 1.

Burlington Clipper. "Colchester." January 27, 1900, 1.

———. "Mr. Editor." February 24, 1900, 6.

———. "News of the State." December 2, 1899, 2.

———. "Queen City Park: And Ideal Camping Place and Summer Resort." April 15, 1897, 1.

Burlington Daily News. "Our New Road." March 1, 1899, 8.

Burlington Daily Sentinel. "Brief Mention." October 17, 1874, 3.

———. "Dawn." October 5, 1874, 2.

———. "Dawn Valcour Community." June 2, 1875, 2.

———. "Shipman vs. Wilcox and White." June 17, 1875, 3.

Burlington Free Press. "Colchester." September 21, 1874, 3.

———. "Colonel Wilcox." November 9, 1874, 3.

———. "Communication from Mr. Shipman." February 15, 1875, 3.

———. "The Dawn Valcour Community." June 12, 1875, 3.

———. "Governor Roosevelt to Have Special Escorts in Vermont." September 6, 1932, 2.

———. "Grand Isle." June 7, 1899, 7.

———. "A *Herald* Correspondent Among the Afinites." September 24, 1874, 2.

———. "Injured by Blast." June 2, 1900, 1.

———. "An Italian Quarrel." February 26, 1900, 6.

———. "Killed." March 10, 1871, 3.

———. "A Narrow Escape." September 4, 1902, 1.

———. "Over the Lake." January 19, 1875, 3.

———. "President Coming to Vermont." June 16, 1902, 2.

———. "President Here." September 1, 1902, 2.

———. "Record Crowd at Middlebury Fair." August 30, 1912, 2.

———. "Remembering Queen City Park." September 25, 1983, 82–84.

———. "The Rutland-Canadian." April 12, 1899, 6.

———. "South Hero." January 31, 1900, 3.

———. "A Strange Piece of News." September 1, 1874, 2.

———. "Vermont and Canada Railroad." August 26, 1850, 2.

———. "Motorboat Patrol on Lake Champlain Seizes 1,200 Bottles of Bear." June 6, 1925, 1.

———. "Supposed Rum Runner Found in Otter Creek." August 17, 1932, 6.

Burlington Free Press and Times. "Fire Destroys 13 Queen City Park Buildings; Loss $100,000." May 18, 1939, 16.

Burlington Local News. "Earth." July 29, 1899, 8.

Burlington Vermont: Early 20th Century Postcard Views. https://www.uvm.edu/~hp206/2012/bosworth/sailingcanal.html.

Burlington Weekly Free Press. "Dawn Valcour Community." February 12, 1875, 3.

———. "The New Free Love Enterprise on Lake Champlain." September 11, 1874, 4.

Catholic Union and Times. "Last of Summer School." August 31, 1899, 1.

Champlain History Center. "The Canal Boat Industry in the Village of Champlain." http://www.champlainhistory.org/canal-boat-industry.html.

Cohn, Arthur, and Marshall True. "The Wreck of the *General Butler* and the Mystery of Lake Champlain's Sailing Canal Boats." Vermont History Journal (1992): 29–43.

Coolidge, Guy Omeron. *The French Occupation of the Champlain Valley from 1609 to 1759.* Fleischmanns, NY: Purple Mountains Press, 1999.

Crisman, Kevin. "Vermont's Steamboat Pioneer Captain Sherman of Vergennes." *Vermont History Journal* 86, no. 2 (Summer/Fall 2018): 95–131.

Daily Journal. "State Matters." November 23, 1969, 3.

Democrat and Chronicle. "Delightful Day at Bluff Point." August 4, 1897, 1.

———. "McKinley's Sunday." August 2, 1897, 2.

———. "Mrs. McKinley Better." August 18, 1899, 5.

———. "Mrs. McKinley Much Better." July 29, 1899, 2.

———. "President at the Garrison." August 17, 1897, 1.

Democrat and Weekly Sentinel. "Dawn Valcour Community." January 16, 1875, 2.

Earth. "Grand Isle." October 21, 1899, 4.

Elizabethtown Post. "Masonic Convention at Keeseville." October 5, 1922, 1.

Enterprise and Vermonter. "Over the State." February 17, 1899, 6.

Founders Online. "Thomas Jefferson to Martha Jefferson Randolph, 31 May 1791." National Archives. Accessed November 26, 2022. https://founders.archives.gov/documents/Jefferson/01-20-02-0173-0006.

FreightWaves. https://www.freightwaves.com/news/freightwaves-classics-infrastructure-champlain-canal-opened-the-champlain-valley-to-settlers-and-commerce.

Hallowell, Laura. "The Story of Lake Champlain." In *Lake Champlain: An Illustrated History.* Jay, NY: Adirondack Life, 2009.

Hamilton College. "The Commercial Era of the 1800s: The Sailing Canal Boat *General Butler.*" https://courses.hamilton.edu/lake-champlain-warships/sailing-canal-boat-general-butler#prettyPhoto.

Hornellsville Weekly Tribune. "Visited Fort Ethan Allen." August 6, 1897, 1.

Jones, Richard C. *The Central Vermont Railway.* Vol. 1. *1830–1886.* Silverton, CO: Sundance Publications Limited, 1981.

Kane, Adam, and Chris Sabick. "Barge (Wreck OO)." Lake Champlain Maritime Museum. https://www.lcmm.org/archaeology/shipwrecks/barge-wreck-oo/.

———. "Lake Champlain Underwater Cultural Resources Survey—Volume IV: 1999 Results and Volume V: 2000 Results." Lake Champlain Maritime Museum. 2001 https://core.tdar.org/document/253059/lake-champlain-underwater-cultural-resources-survey-volume-iv-1999-results-and-volume-v-2000-results.

———. "Port Henry Drawboat." Lake Champlain Maritime Museum. https://www.lcmm.org/archaeology/shipwrecks/port-henry-drawboat/.

———. "Rouses Point Barge Wreck." Lake Champlain Maritime Museum. https://www.lcmm.org/archaeology/shipwrecks/rouses-point-barge-wreck-ww/.

Kane, Adam I., Christopher Sabick and Sara Brigadier. "Lake Champlain Underwater Cultural Resources Survey—Volume VI: 2001 Results and Volume VII: 2002 Results." Lake Champlain Maritime Museum. 2002. https://core.tdar.org/document/390910/lake-champlain-underwater-cultural-resources-survey-volume-vi-2001-results-and-volume-vii-2002-results.

———. "Steel Barge (Wreck FFF) VT-GI-29." Lake Champlain Maritime Museum. https://www.lcmm.org/archaeology/shipwrecks/steel-barge-wreck-fff-vt-gi-29/.

Kingsley, Stephen, and Ronald Astmann. "The Burleigh Brothers: 19th Century Titans of the Champlain Basin." *Journal of Vermont History* (Summer/Fall 2000): 185–96.

Knight, George. *A Search for Identity*. Rocky Hill, CT: Review and Herald Publications, 2000.

Lake Champlain Maritime Museum. "Horse Ferry." https://www.lcmm.org/archaeology/vermont-underwater-historic-preserves/horse-ferry/.

———. "Rouses Point Barge (Wreck WW)." https://www.lcmm.org/archaeology/shipwrecks/rouses-point-barge-wreck-ww/

———. "Sailing Boat *General Butler*." https://www.lcmm.org/archaeology/vermont-underwater-historic-preserves/sailing-canal-boat-general-butler/.

———. "Shipwreck Tour: *General Butler*." https://www.lcmm.org/shipwreck-tour-general-butler/

———. "Steamboat *Champlain II*." https://www.lcmm.org/archaeology/vermont-underwater-historic-preserves/steamboat-champlain-ii/.

———. "War of 1812 Wrecks." https://www.lcmm.org/archaeology/shipwrecks/war-of-1812-wrecks/.

Lake Champlain Underwater Cultural Resources Survey—Volume VIII: 2003 Results and Volume IX: 2004 Results. Adam I. Kane, A. Peter Barranco, Joanne M. DellaSalla, Sarah E. Lyman, Christopher R. Sabick. Vergennes, VT: Lake Champlain Maritime Museum, 2007 (tDAR id: 391001); doi:10.6067/XCV8G73GBB.

Lake Placid News. "Hotel Ausable Open with Banquet." June 30, 1922, 14.

Landmark. "State of Vermont." March 2, 1900, 7.

Lee, David. "The Contest for Isle Aux Noix 1759–1760." *Vermont Historical Society Journal* 99 (Spring 1969).

Lyndonville Journal. "Chittenden County." March 12, 1875, 1.

———. "Chittenden County." March 26, 1875, 1.

Mazowita, Sophie. "Red Rocks Park: Working Towards a Community-Based Management Plan." UVM Field Naturalist Program for the City of South Burlington. April 2023. https://cms6.revize.com/revize/southburlington/document_center/RecsParks/RedRocks.ManagementStudy.pdf.

Middlebury People's Press. "The Imposters." December 6, 1842, 2.

———. "Millerism." November 15, 1842, 3.

———. "The Millerites." January 18, 1843, 3.

Middlebury Register. "Addison County." May 2, 1871, 2.

———. "Addison County." November 28, 1871, 3.

———. "The Addison Railroad." January 17, 1871, 3.

———. "A Glance Over the State." November 24, 1899.

———. "A Glance Over the State." February 16, 1900, 1.

———. "The Rutland Wins." December 29, 1899, 1.

———. "Town Meeting." February 8, 1870, 3.

Miller, William. Letter to Joshua V. Himes. February 4, 1844.

Montpelier Evening Argus. "President Arrives." August 30, 1902, 1.

———. "Vermont News Items." December 29, 1899, 2.

National Weather Service. "Lake Champlain Extremes and Level." https://www.weather.gov/btv/lakeLevel?year=2023.

News and Advertiser. "State of Vermont." May 16, 1899.

News and Citizen. "Dawn Valcour Community." April 22, 1875, 2.

———. "Dawn Valcour Community." April 26, 1875, 2.

———. "Valcour Community." March 18, 1875.

———. "The Vermont Utah." February 18, 1875, 2.

New York Daily Herald. "The Free Lovers." September 21, 1874, 3.

———. "More Social Madness." October 24, 1874.

———. "The Valcourians." October 27, 1874, 4.

New York Times. "The *New York Times* Illustrated Magazine." August 13, 1899, 25.
———. "The President Horrified." August 9, 1897, 2.
———. "President Reviews Troops." August 19, 1899, 5.
———. "The President's Summer Home." July 30, 1897, 5.
———. "The President's Vacation." August 13, 1899, 3.
———. "Root Goes to Plattsburgh." August 22, 1899, 4.
———. "Schurman Wants to Be Heard." August 23, 1899, 2.
———. "What Is Doing in Society." August 18, 1899, 7.
New York Tribune. "The *Boston Post* Says." December 22, 1842, 1.
———. "Cheers for the President." August 7, 1897, 7.
———. "The President's Outing." August 1, 1897, 7.
———. "The President's Rest." July 31, 1897, 7.
———. "The President's Sunday." August 2, 1897, 7.
———. "The President's Vacation." August 1, 1899, 6.
North Star. "Good Fruits." January 9, 1843, 3.
———. "Spiritualist Camp Meeting." July 20, 1883, 3.
O'Connor, Kevin. "Hail to the Chiefs." *Barre Times Argus*, March 25, 2012, 1.
Payne, Stephen. "Memorial: Orlando Kellog Jr." Find a Grave. March 11, 2011. https://www.findagrave.com/memorial/66761729/orlando-kellogg.
Plattsburgh Daily Press. "Lake Patrol Seize Two Motor Boats." June 13, 1932.
———. "Local News Items." November 17, 1899, 6.
Plattsburgh Republican. September 10, 1842, 3.
———. "Babcock's Body Still in the Lake." August 19, 1931.
———. "Babcock's Body Still Not Recovered." August 20, 1931.
———. "Lake Champlain." August 1899.
———. "Lake Patrol Seize Yacht Near Island." June 11, 1929.
———. "The Line of Boats." December 14, 1850, 2.
———. "Northern Railroad." October 19, 1850, 3.
———. "Officer While Fishing Spots Ale Laden Boat." October 31, 1931.
———. "1,000 Cases of Ale Seized on Canal Boat." August 20, 1932, 3.
———. "Rum Boat Has Not Yet Been Found." August 15, 1932, 3.
———. "Rumrunner Knocks into Lake with Baseball Bat." August 13, 1932, 3.
———. "Seize Five Booze Cars on Vermont." September 4, 1928.
———. "Supposed Rum Boat Is Found." August 18, 1932, 3.
———. "Willsboro Man Caught on Booze Laden Bough." May 11, 1932.
Plattsburgh Sentinel. "Barge of Hay Being Held by Customs Men." August 19, 1927, 6.
———. "Paragrams." December 22, 1899, 1.

———. "U.S. Officers Face Problem on Lake Champlain." May 13, 1927.

Preservation Trust of Vermont. "1903–1956: The Island Villa Hotel." January 1, 2006. https://ptvermont.org/1903-1956-the-island-villa-hotel/.

Richford Gazette. December 22, 1899, 2.

Rogers, Tom. "History Space: Vermont's Great Outdoors." *Burlington Free Press.* November 11, 2017. https://www.burlingtonfreepress.com/story/news/2017/11/11/history-space-vermonts-great-outdoors/107390612/.

Rowe, David. *God's Strange Work.* Grand Rapids, MI: William B. Eerdman's Publishing Company, 2008.

Rutland Daily Globe. "Addison County Railroad." January 5, 1870, 3.

———. "Addison Railroad." November 7, 1870, 3.

———. "Addison Railroad." September 27, 1871, 3.

———. "The Dawn Valcour Community." September 17, 1874, 1.

———. "Good Bye, Valcour." November 29, 1875, 3.

———. "Middlebury." May 16, 1871, 2.

———. "New Railroad Projects." March 9, 1871, 4.

———. "The Ticonderoga Bridge and the Addison County Railroad." February 9, 1871, 1.

———. "Two Men Buried Alive." January 26, 1871, 5.

———. "The Valcour Difficulty." March 16, 1875, 2.

———. "Vermont Affairs." March 3, 1875, 3.

———. "Vermont Notes." November 24, 1874, 4.

Saint Albans Daily Messenger. August 2, 1875, 3.

———. July 21, 1880, 3.

———. November 29, 1975, 3.

———. "A Day at Missisquoi Park." July 21, 1880, 3.

———. "End of the Dawn Valcour Community." November 9, 1875, 2.

———. "Free Conferences." October 3, 1874, 4.

———. "Grand Isle." December 20, 1899.

———. "Grand Isle." April 16, 1900, 7.

———. "Grand Isle." May 23, 1900, 2.

———. "May Be Bunker Hill Gun." May 11, 1909.

———. "Over the Lake." March 1, 1875, 2.

———. "Painsville and Campbellburgh." March 28, 1850, 2.

———. "Roosevelt the Guest of Honor." September 6, 1901, 2.

———. "St. Albans and Vicinity." December 3, 1875.

———. "The Valcour Community." March 12, 1875, 3.

———. "Williston." August 2, 1875, 3.

Saint Albans Messenger. "Stepped Out Too Soon." May 24, 1900, 2.

Saint Albans Weekly Messenger. "Bridge at Rouses Point." November 7, 1850, 2.

———. "Central Vermont Railroad!" February 20, 1851, 1.

———. "Visit of the Vermont Legislature to Rouses Point." October 31, 1850, 2.

Saint Anne's Shrine. "Our History." https://www.saintannesshrine.org/history.

Sayers, Kaylee. "Saint Anne's Shrine: A Well-Established Piece of Saint Michael's Life History." July 7, 2022. https://www.smcvt.edu/about-smc/news/2022/july/saint-annes-shrine-a-well-established-piece-of-saint-michaels-life-history/.

Schneider, Janet. "Looking Back: Queen City Park." Other Paper, November 19, 2019. https://www.vtcng.com/otherpapersbvt/community/looking-back-queen-city-park/article_3872d88f-4a4a-5280-ada7-587d8718b3b3.html.

Sentinel and Democrat. "A Millerite." July 29, 1842, 1.

Sheldon Historical Society. "The Springs." https://sheldonvthistorical.org/the-springs/.

Sherman, Michael, Gene Sessions and P. Jeffrey Potash. *Freedom and Unity: A History of Vermont.* Barre: Vermont Historical Society, 2004.

Spirit of the Age. "A Good Joke." September 9, 1842, 4.

———. "State at Large." April 27, 1871, 3.

———. "Vermont Railroads." December 5, 1850, 2.

Standard Union. "Callers on the President." August 9, 1899, 5.

———. "Hereaux's Death Confirmed." July 27, 1899, 1.

———. "McKinley Invited." August 15, 1899, 5.

———. "Pass in Review." August 3, 1897, 5.

———. "Vice President Hobart Ill." August 5, 1899, 1.

Star Gazette. "At Hotel Champlain." July 29, 1897, 1.

———. "McKinley's Guests." August 1, 1899, 7.

Sun. "The President's Vacation." August 13, 1899, 2.

Swanton Courier. "About Town." September 13, 1895, 3.

———. "Finds Big Cannonball." July 18, 1918, 1.

———. "The Original Hotel Champlain." June 26, 1913, 8.

———. "South Hero." June 15, 1899, 4.

Swanton Historical Society. "An Outline of Swanton's History." https://swantonhistoricalsociety.org/swanton-history/.

Texas A&M University. "The Canal Boat Wrecks of Lake Champlain." Nautical Archeology Program. https://liberalarts.tamu.edu/nautarch/nwl/lake-champlain-projects/lccanalboats/.

Ticonderoga Sentinel. "Close Navigation on Lake Champlain Friday." December 5, 1929.

———. "Seize Rowboat with 240 Quarts of Ale." August 2, 1928, 2.

Uhl, Jerry. "Recollections of the Westport Inn: 1930 through 1950." Ballard Park: Westport, NY. https://www.ballardparkny.org/history.

Universalist Watchman. "Insanity by Millerism." December 24, 1842, 2.

———. "Millerism." July 9, 1842, 2.

———. "Millerism vs Abolitionism." July 23, 1842, 2.

———. "More Fruits of Millerism." January 28, 1843, 3.

———. "A Question Answered." August 13, 1842, 2.

———. "Signs of the 2nd Coming." January 7, 1843.

University of Vermont Silver Special Collections Library. "Queen City Park Association Records: Historical Note." https://scfindingaids.uvm.edu/resources/queencityparkassociation#.

UVM Landscape Change Program. https://glcp.uvm.edu/landscape_new/dating/boats/canal_barges.php.

Vermont Chronicle. "The Valcour Community." September 19, 1874, 4.

Vermont Historical Society. "Researching Lake Champlain Celebrations at the Vermont Historical Society." *Vermont History Journal* 143 (Summer/Fall 2009).

Vermont Mercury. "A Singular Phenomenon." January 6, 1843, 2.

———. "Wonderful Sights in the Air." February 17, 1843, 3.

Vermont Patriot and State Gazette. "Millerism." December 3, 1843, 3.

Vermont Phoenix. "Fish and Game League." September 13, 1901, 2.

———. "Monthly Mis. of Religion and Letters." November 25, 1842, 2.

———. "Operated from Rutland." January 20, 1899, 4.

———. "Rutland-Canadian R.R." April 7, 1899, 3

Vermont Religious Observer. "Another Sign." February 14, 1843, 3.

Vermont Standard. "Addison County." November 3, 1870, 3.

———. "State at Large." October 1, 1874, 3.

———. "State at Large." February 18, 1875, 2.

Vermont Statesman. "Daily Number of Attendees." September 28, 1842, 3.

Vermont Watchman and State Journal. "Chittenden County." October 13, 1875, 3.

———. "The Manufacture and Builder." February 22, 1871, 2.

Walton's Daily Journal. "The Excursion." November 1, 1850, 2.

Wickman, Don. *Strong Ground: Mount Independence and the American Revolution*. Orwell, VT: Mount Independence Coalition, 2017.

Williams, Donald R. *Adirondack Hotels and Inns*. Charleston, SC: Arcadia Publishing, 2008.

Wiseman, Frederick M. *Seven Sisters: Ancient Seeds and Food Systems of the Wabanaki People and the Chesapeake Bay Region*. Ontario: Earth Haven Learning Centre Inc., 2018.

Woodstock Post. "Chittenden County." March 19, 1875, 1.

———. "Mrs. Oren Shipman." April 16, 1875, 1.

World. "Hobart Joins McKinley." August 4, 1897, 7.

———. "McKinley in Vermont." August 4, 1897, 7.

Yonkers Herald. "A Day of Pleasure." August 15, 1899, 7.

———. "McKinley to Summer at Champlain." July 20, 1899, 2.

———. "The President's Rest." August 2, 1899, 4.

About the Authors

The married couple of Jason Barney and Christine Eldred have brought you the *Hidden History of Lake Champlain*. They loved doing the research together and hope you enjoyed the book.

JASON BARNEY has published three books: *Northern Vermont and the War of 1812*, *The Hidden History of Franklin County* and *Northern Vermont and the Revolutionary War*, all with The History Press. He has been working at Missisquoi Valley Union High School for twenty-one years. He was the VFW Local Teacher of the Year in 2020. He was the MVU Teacher in 2021 and was one of the semifinalists for Vermont Teacher of the Year in 2022. He was the recipient of the Victor R. Swenson Humanities Council Award for Excellence in Teaching in 2019. Jason served in the Vermont legislature from 1997 to 2002 and served as vice-chair of the Education Committee for two years. In 2021, Jason administered a prestigious National Endowment for the Humanities Grant with the Vermont Archaeological Society on Revolutionary War sites in Vermont. He is the current president of the

Swanton Historical Society. In 2023, Jason was awarded Gilder Lehrman/Vermont State History Teacher of the Year.

Christine Eldred is a librarian, genealogist and writer. She has a bachelor's degree in English literature from Middlebury College, an MLIS from Syracuse University and a certificate in genealogical research from Boston University. She's worked in a variety of roles in schools, nonprofits, government offices and libraries. Christine has published several articles, chapters and guides to preserving and defending intellectual freedom in school libraries and has presented at local and national library conferences. As a professional genealogist, she hosts workshops and works with clients on family history research and dual citizenship applications. With social history as a lens, Christine is interested in understanding how culture, community and historical events shape the choices our ancestors made and how our ancestors' lives continue to affect us today.

The Capital of the North

Lake Champlain is one of America's most historic waterways, but much of its history has remained hidden. With the arrival of Europeans, the lake became a vital route between the English in New England and the French in Quebec. Its isolated beauty contrasted sharply with the bloody military campaigns that unfolded there. While enormous forts were erected, colonial villages blossomed and eighteenth-century naturalist Peter Kalm spread the word of its bucolic charm. William Miller attracted large audiences as he preached that the world would end in the 1840s. Valcour Island developed its own commune, and when Prohibition took effect, the towns near the Canadian border became hotbeds of bootlegging. From presidential visits to shipwrecks, local authors Jason Barney and Christine Eldred chronicle some of the lake's lesser-known contributions to American history.

$24.99

MADE
IN THE
USA

ISBN 978-1-4671-5725-4

52499